Praise for *Tattoo Magick*

"*Tattoo Magick* not only explains, but also directs on constructing, empowering, energizing, and making even more sacred the very symbols we use to mark our skin."
—**ELWYNN THE WITCH**, author of *Between the Horns*

"A must have for any witchy tattoo lover!"
—**MANDI EM**, author of *Witchcraft Therapy*

"A powerful bridge between the culturally tied tattooing of the past and the magic of marking the flesh in the present."
—**REBECCA BEYER**, author of *Wild Witchcraft*

"*Tattoo Magick* is pure art."
—**MORGAN MOSS**, owner of Inked Goddess Creations (IG: @inkedgoddesscreations)

"A wonderful book to help everyone evolve spiritually and attain their goals."
—**LISA STARDUST**, author of *The Astrology Deck*

"Jake's book is a rarity, providing thought-provoking advice."
—**LAURA TEMPEST ZAKROFF**, author of *Sigil Witchery*

"A spellbinding fusion of artistry, devotion, and power."
—**MICHAEL HERKES**, author of *The GLAM Witch*

"A well-researched, well-written book."
—**MELISSA CYNOVA**, author of *Kitchen Table Tarot*

"A powerful exploration of tattooing."
—**CAROLINE LINDSKOV**, tattoo artist, Miss Kali Tattoos (IG: @misskalitattoos)

"As someone who has used tattoos to heal by covering my body in inked prayer, I found this beautiful book incredibly inspiring."
—**DAMIEN ECHOLS**, author of *Life After Death*

"*Tattoo Magick* dives deep into the sacred power of ink."
—**THERESA REED, "The Tarot Lady,"** author of *The Book of Astrological Returns*

"A must-read book for the curious, the inked, and the magically inclined."
—**RICHARD WEBSTER**, best-selling author of over one hundred books

"*Tattoo Magick* brings insight through experience and thought-provoking reflections for tapping into the power and potential of the ancient and transformative art of tattooing."
—**COBY MICHAEL**, author of the Poison Path series

"An intriguing and in-depth look at the way that tattoos can be woven into spirituality and become more than just ink in skin."
—**MORGAN DAIMLER**, author of *Fairy* and *Pantheon: The Irish*

"*Tattoo Magick* is a long overdue gem."
—**TESS WHITEHURST**, author of *The Halloween Forever Oracle*

"An incredibly thorough, magickal guide."
—**NIKKI WARDWELL SLEATH**, author of *Dream Sorcery*

"A thorough and magickal exploration of tattooing from a modern witchcraft context."
—**PHOENIX LEFAE**, author of *Spirit Magic*

"This book shows how tattoos can be empowered and activated to achieve willed purposes in ritual magic."
—**DONALD TYSON**, author of the critically acclaimed Necronomicon series

"This well-researched and clearly written book explores the profound layers of tattooing as more than decoration."
—**AMY ZERNER & MONTE FARBER**, authors of *The Enchanted Tarot*

"An insightful and practical guide to working with tattoos as vessels of intention, history, and power."
—**JEN SANKEY**, author of *Manifesting by the Moon*

"Jake writes with both scholarship and soul, weaving history and modern witchcraft into something deeply personal and empowering."
—**MONICA CROSSON**, author of *Wild Magical Soul*

"A refreshing, wise, and in-depth book."
—**RAVEN DIGITALIS**, author of *Shadow Magick Spellbook*

"If you want to mix magic with your ink, this is the book for you."
—**DEBORAH BLAKE**, author of *Everyday Witch's Book of Deities*

"*Tattoo Magick* welcomes you to explore how tattoos can become powerful, living symbols of intention, healing, devotion, and personal transformation."
—**ETHONY DAWN**, author of *Become an Exceptional Tarot Reader*

"Jake walks us through the art of choosing a magical tattoo, empowering it, and using it to manifest our desires."
—**CHRIS ALLAUN**, author of *The Queer Spirit Worker*

"Jake Morningstar draws upon a continuum of magical, spiritual, and devotional traditions to inspire a practice anchored in the modern day."
—**MHARA STARLING**, author of *Welsh Witchcraft*

"Every part of our life can be enhanced by, and serve, our magick; a truth exemplified in *Tattoo Magick*."
—**ANTHONY RELLA**, author of *Slow Magic*

"A unique and standout book."
—**CHRIS CARTER**, magickal tattoo artist and Chaos Gnostic practitioner (IG: @cursecartertattoos)

"An excellent guide to help you enhance your magick in a way you may never have considered."
—**STEPHANIE WOODFIELD**, author of *Call of the Morrigan Oracle*

"Jake Morningstar shares creative and powerful ways of working with tattoos in magic."
—**DURGADAS ALLON DURIEL**, author of *The Little Work*

"A wealth of knowledge for anyone who has a tattoo or is interested in getting one."
—**ASTREA TAYLOR**, author of *Intuitive Witchcraft* and *Air Magic*

"A groundbreaking new approach to magick that deserves a place on every practitioner's shelf."
—**DANIELLE BLACKWOOD**, author of *The Twelve Faces of the Goddess*

"For anyone trying to pin down the 'I know this is magical but how to do it' thought, this book is for you!"
—**DEBRA BURRIS**, author of *Weather Magic*

"Morningstar provides a structured framework for intention, symbolism, and ritual."
—**NATAN ALEXANDER**, tattoo artist, Witch City Ink & Star and Snake (IG: @natanink)

"Anyone and everyone can gain new and fantastic ideas from reading this book."
—**STACEY LYNNE STEWART**, coauthor, *Heathen Traditions of the Pennsylvania Dutch*

"Jake Morningstar offers thoughtful practices and rituals for working intentionally with tattoos."
—**CELESTE LARSEN**, author of *Heal the Witch Wound*

"Original and empowering."
—**ELLIOT ADAM**, best-selling author of *Fearless Tarot*

"A FANTASTIC companion for Witches (and all magickal folk) interested in adorning their body with the art of tattoo!"
—**MULYSA MAYHEM**, magickal tattoo artist (IG: @mulysamayhem)

"A fascinating exploration of the magick of tattoos."
—**CYNDI BRANNEN**, author of *Keeping Her Keys*

"Jake Morningstar's compelling ideas and thought-provoking concepts are presented in an approachable and comprehensive way."
—**DREE AMANDI PIKE**, author of *The Art of Aromatherapy in Magick*

"Jake Morningstar gives us a precious gift in the form of this book."
—**PRIESTESS STEPHANIE ROSE BIRD**, author of *365 Days of Hoodoo*

"This book is an essential addition to your library."
—**JAIME GIRONÉS**, author of *Llewellyn's Little Book of the Day of the Dead*

"A powerful exploration of what it means to embody your spiritual practice—literally."
—**ALY KRAVETZ**, founder of BetterWitch Coaching

"Bold, rebellious, and layered in artistic meaning."
—**TOMÁS PROWER**, author of *La Santa Muerte*

"Jake Morningstar shows that tattooing can be much more than just ink on skin."
—**JACK CHANEK**, author of *Tarot for the Magically Inclined*

TATTOO MAGICK

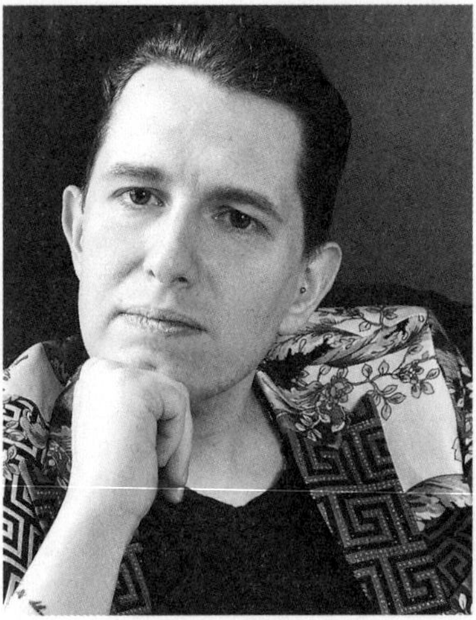

© Jake Morningstar

About the Author

Jake Morningstar, the founder and high priest of Diamond Eye coven, has been a Witch for over twenty years. A true believer in learning (eleven years!), Jake has a BS in neuroscience from Brown and a PhD in marketing from Wharton. He has taught hundreds in the mundane and esoteric arts. Visit him at @that_morningstar_witch on Instagram.

TATTOO MAGICK

Drawing on New and Old Ink for Spells and Spiritual Connections

Jake Morningstar

LLEWELLYN
WOODBURY, MINNESOTA

FIRST EDITION
First Printing, 2026

Book design by Donna Burch-Brown
Cover design by Shannon McKuhen
Interior art by the Llewellyn Art Department

Library of Congress Cataloging-in-Publication Data

Names: Morningstar, Jake author
Title: Tattoo magick : drawing on new and old ink for spells and spiritual connections / by Jake Morningstar.
Description: First edition. | Woodbury, MN : Llewellyn Publications, a division of Llewellyn Worldwide Ltd, 2026. | Includes bibliographical references and index. | Summary: "New, old, temporary, or still in the design phase, any tattoo can be a powerful conduit for your workings. Learn how to set up spells during your tattooing session, discover how pain can be harnessed for power, and explore what magick you can do with preexisting tattoos"— Provided by publisher.
Identifiers: LCCN 2026021037 (print) | LCCN 2026021038 (ebook) | ISBN 9780738783161 trade paperback | ISBN 9780738783246 ebook
Subjects: LCSH: Magic | Tattooing | Witchcraft | LCGFT: Trivia and miscellanea.
Classification: LCC BF1621 .M676 2026 (print) | LCC BF1621 (ebook)
LC record available at https://lccn.loc.gov/2026021037
LC ebook record available at https://lccn.loc.gov/2026021038

Llewellyn Publications
A Division of Llewellyn Worldwide Ltd.
2143 Wooddale Drive
Woodbury, MN 55125-2989
www.llewellyn.com

Printed in the United States of America

GPSR Representation:
UPI-2M PLUS d.o.o., Medulićeva 20, 10000 Zagreb, Croatia
matt.parsons@upi2mbooks.hr

To Jay and Ash
for their unwavering support

To Elysia
for taking a chance

To that twelve-year-old baby Witch
who would have lost his shit if he only knew

Contents

Disclaimer

Tattooing is a procedure that you elect to receive at your own risk. There are inherent risks involved, and outcomes can vary. No party associated with the writing, publishing, distribution, or sale of this book is liable for any injuries, complications, or adverse effects that may occur before, during, or after the procedure.

The parties associated with the writing, publishing, distribution, and sale of this book do not endorse self-harm, unsafe practices, or illegal conduct. Readers are urged to prioritize safety at all times.

For Any Readers Who Don't Already Have a Tattoo or Don't Already Practice Magick

Welcome! So nice to have you! I figure some of you might be interested in this book not because you practice magick but because you have tattoos and the idea of magick is intriguing. Conversely, you might be a magickal practitioner who wants to get a tattoo. Maybe you are neither! Either way, you are about to embark on one of the most fulfilling and empowering journeys of your life.

If you haven't gotten a tattoo before, I hope this book is the catalyst for you to take the plunge. Tattoos are not something to be entered into too lightly, though. They are permanent, after all. So, feel free to take all the time you need to come up with the design and find a good tattoo artist. But don't worry: While you are working up to your first tattoo, you can read the final chapter of this book. It will give you ideas for magick you can make with temporary forms of body decoration. If one of the reasons you've held off on getting a tattoo is the pain, I highly recommend reading my chapter "The Power in Pain." Hopefully it will help show you that the pain is not necessarily a bad thing; in fact it might be the coolest part of a spell you make in the tattooing session.

If you haven't practiced magick before, I should say, as a point of warning, that this is not a magick 101 book. In my mind, a good 101 book lays the foundation for you to work with a wide variety of types of magick. As versatile as the practice is that's the subject of this book, it is only one class of magick. So, I've written this assuming the reader has some magickal experience. That doesn't mean you have to set this book down, though. The glossary will help explain any of the magickal concepts you come across. But I do recommend you read a 101 book. I have several recommendations here:

- *Psychic Witch: A Metaphysical Guide to Meditation, Magick & Manifestation* by Mat Auryn
- *Ritual: An Essential Grimoire* by Damien Echols and Lorri Davis
- *The Witch's Book of Spellcraft: A Practical Guide to Connecting with the Magick of Candles, Crystals, Plants & Herbs* by Jason Mankey, Matt Cavalli, Amanda Lynn, and Ari Mankey
- *To Ride a Silver Broomstick: New Generation Witchcraft* by Silver RavenWolf

Bon voyage and blessed be!

Introduction

Did you know about one in three people in the United States has at least one tattoo? And two out of three people with tattoos will get more than one.[1] If you have a tattoo, or are even thinking of getting a tattoo, you are in good company. If you're a magickal practitioner, you are especially in good company. Go to any Pagan gathering and you will see quite a few people with ink on their bodies. So many people get tattoos as a form of self-expression, and Witches are very self-expressive. A lot of us are creatives. A lot of us are completely unafraid of our uniqueness, and want it to be known. A lot of us discover that magick gives us the agency to be who we are in a repressive, marginalizing environment. Now that we are free, we want to share ourselves with the world. If you don't have a tattoo but are considering one, make the decision at your own pace, but know you are surrounded by people who understand. If some people say tattoos are for freaks, we all say louder, "Let your freak flag fly!"

Consider why you got that tattoo you have or why you want to get your first tattoo. Sometimes, maybe often, it's a meaningful and personal reason. Maybe it is celebrating something you've done or reminding you of a habit you don't want to do. Maybe it highlights

---

1. Schaeffer and Dinesh, "32% of Americans Have a Tattoo."

something you love about yourself or a quality you want to bring out. Maybe it is a reminder of a loved one or someone you've lost. What if you could tap into that meaning and enhance it? What if you could use your tattoo to achieve more of the things you celebrate or to reprogram bad habits? Use it to enhance the characteristic you love and get that quality or feeling you want more of? Use it to connect with your loved ones on a deeper level? In other words, what if you could turn that tattoo into magick?

It might escape a magickal practitioner or two that tattoos have powerful parallels with magick. Personal symbols connected to powerful need—even getting something because it looked cool is fulfilling a need—is a valid description of tattoos. It also describes the props we use to focus in magick. It can also describe the object of the magick, the outcome we visualize and the object that we enchant to draw upon later. Tattoos, then, are vessels through which we can express our magickal will if we so choose. The act of tattooing is a spell waiting to be harnessed.

Like most people who get tattoos, ever since I was little, I craved self-expression and self-empowerment. I wanted to be myself, to be unique, to successfully stand up to the bullies who picked on me for being different. As a gay person in the '90s/'00s—and someone whose mental health weighed him down—this was hard. But it meant that every trial and tribulation I faced successfully, with or without magick, was something to be celebrated. One day, that took the form of a small tattoo on my hip. It was a celebration of recovering from an eating disorder and a reminder to not let it happen again. It stayed in secret while I was living with a parent who did not approve. Every time I was able to get a peek at it, though, I felt a little happier, a little more like myself.

Four years later, shortly after moving out, I got my entire left chest tattooed. Fourteen triangles, each representing an event I found especially traumatic. I am of the opinion that what doesn't kill you lands you in therapy. It does not make you stronger. But I hoped seeing what I had gone through would give me faith I could withstand future trials. So, I tattooed.

To be honest, I picked triangles because out of all the markings I made on my skin with a permanent marker, they looked the coolest. No deep symbolism with that, just pure aesthetic expression. In fact, triangles do not stand for hope in any magickal system, nor do they stand for strength. Most often, triangles are in symbols for protection and banishment, and the number three in numerology typically stands for creativity and communication. What I found over time, though, was when I was planning the placement of multiple candles in a spell, often I would put them in a triangle. Not in spells for banishment or protection or communication. They showed up in spells where I needed strength. I found the exact same thing when I started making sigils out of shapes instead of letters, a practice I began thanks to Laura Tempest Zakroff's life-changing book *Sigil Witchery*. Whenever I needed to incorporate strength into a sigil, the triangle was always a shape I thought to add.

What I realized was that I wasn't associating triangles with strength. I was associating my triangle tattoo with strength. My tattoo was showing up in my magick. Now, some people might say that the reason I got the tattoo was at least tangentially to give me strength and an association was made between my tattoo and strength, and the association, being in my mind, made its way into my Witchcraft. Sure. But here's the thing: That connection would not have happened unless it worked, unless the tattoo somehow got past my cynicism about trauma and made me stronger. I had inadvertently cast a spell.

Since the realization that tattoos have power, I have been playing with tattoo magick, experimenting with spells. One tattoo was added to enhance my power and never let me forget it. One tattoo was added to enhance and inspire all of my spellwork. One tattoo was added to provide a space for daily affirmations. Another was added because it just looked cool. Hey, they don't all have to be functional! But even that tattoo, like others that I didn't mention here, was a magickal, sacred act.

I pass the results of my experiments on to you now. This book is a culmination of my workings and my research—not just into tattoos but things that are tattoo adjacent, such as temporary body decoration. I have tried to be pretty comprehensive across the thirteen chapters of this book.

Knowing that tattoo magick is not very widespread, at least in our country, I start with a look at the historical and modern intersection of tattoos and spirituality around the world. I hope that this will bring to life the power of tattooing, which we can work with using the system of magick we practice. After that is the chapter you all came for: "The Ways Healed Tattoos Can Be Used in Magick." But magick is not the only spiritual use for tattoos, so I focus the third chapter on using tattoos for spiritual devotions and the fourth on ancestor work.

At this point, we transition from healed tattoos to new tattoos. There is nothing saying we can't make more tattoos to do fun magickal things with, and in fact you can even work magick during the tattooing session. We work through it chronologically, though, because there are several steps to a new tattoo. We start with two chapters on designing the tattoo. One of them is going to help you figure out what you want your tattoos to look like in general—your "tattoo aesthetic." Let's be real: You need to design your tattoo for your magick, but you also want a tattoo you'll like to look at since, you know, tattoos are permanent. After that, we get into designing your tattoo for your intention. Then we talk about how to find a tattoo artist; even if you already have someone you like to work with, they aren't guaranteed to be comfortable with magickal tattoos. We also go into magickal timing so you can schedule your tattoo for the perfect moment.

Now we get to the tattoo session. There is a chapter on how to work magick in the tattoo session itself. There are several ways to raise energy during your tattoo, but one that is especially relevant—pain—deserves a special mention. This is because there are documented links between pain and spiritual experiences, making it a particularly powerful sensation to work with. The chapter "The Power in Pain" starts by establishing that link and then covers how to work with it in your tattooing session. Since for most of us spellwork exists within a larger ritual—cleansing and consecrating, casting the magick circle, and so on—there is a chapter on how you make a ritual with the restrictions a tattoo studio places on you. It's not like there will be space for all your magickal tools, for example.

We round out the book with two additional chapters I felt were absolutely necessary. Hopefully, you get a new tattoo and that's it, but not all of us are that lucky. With that in mind, I have a chapter on tattoo touch-ups. The chapter also covers tattoo cover-ups and spell reversals. Finally, tattooing is a permanent body decoration, but no one said a body decoration has to be permanent to have power. You also don't always have the perfect tattoo for the job. So, I go over working magick with some temporary forms of body decoration, such as temporary tattoos and marker.

I look forward to sharing with you this entire book, the result of a hell of a lot of experimentation. And there's no time like the present, is there? Let's begin!

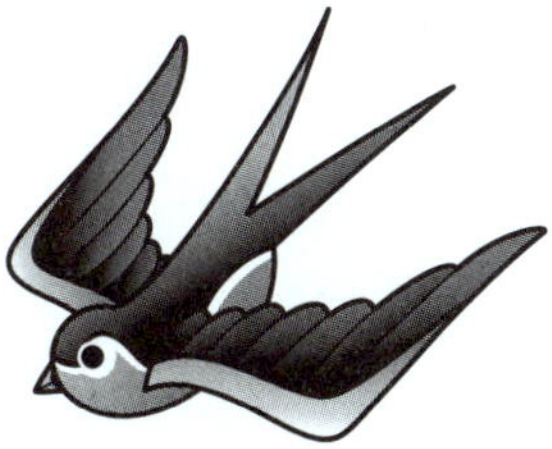

1
The Intersection of Tattoos and Spirituality

Tattoo magick is not a widespread practice, or at least it's not in this country at the time I am writing this. Is that a sign tattoo magick doesn't work? Absolutely not. There are many examples throughout history and around the world of people getting tattoos to bring on spiritual, supernatural powers; interact with deities and spirits; or navigate other realms. Starting this book by telling you about some of them is a great way for you to get acquainted with the power of tattooing so you aren't just taking my word for it. I will not go into great detail because this book is about what you will do with your tattoo using the system of Witchcraft that I and many of you use. It is not about what others have done with theirs. But I hope I have included enough to open your eyes and maybe even spark your curiosity. If you want to know more, I suggest some books at the end of this chapter.

The overlap of tattooing and spirituality goes back thousands of years to one of the earliest known preserved tattoos. A body dating around 2600 BCE was found in 2006 in a place called Rostov Oblast, at the eastern border of Russia and Ukraine. The mummy had a snake tattoo over the shin. That same spot is where the person had a rather nasty fracture that never healed properly. Now, it is known that Indigenous groups in that region, as late as the turn of the twentieth century, believed that snakes corresponded to healing. The snake was used in remedial rituals and placed on healing amulets. It might not be a stretch to say that these are practices that go back a long time with these Indigenous peoples, perhaps even to the time that person was tattooed. Therefore, academics have argued the tattoo was used to channel the power of the snake and heal the man's fractured leg.[2]

Six hundred years after that, we have the first written record of tattooing in ancient Egypt. This occurred in its eleventh dynasty, around 2100–2000 BCE. This is also the dynasty from which some of the earliest Egyptian mummies with tattoos have appeared. The most famous is a priestess of Hathor, goddess of beauty, named Amunet. The purpose of her tattoos is debated. Some believe they were used to treat a hip condition; others believe they were meant to amplify her fertility and beauty. It is significant that the pattern of the dots that make up the tattoo are very similar to markings found on a clay figurine in Eastern Europe. This figurine, which some believe is a goddess, dates to 5000 BCE.[3]

Over the last couple centuries, anthropologists in the Americas, Africa, and Asia have documented several tattoo practices that are spiritual in nature. These include practices of people you'll hear about later in the chapter, such as the Nlaka'pamux in Canada, the Kayabi in the Amazon,[4] and the Ainu in Japan.[5] Thankfully, many of these practices have survived to today or are experiencing a recent revival.

---

2. Shishlina et al.,"Bronze Age Tattoos," 71–72.

3. Rush, *Spiritual Tattoo*, 20–21.

4. Krutak, *Spiritual Skin*, 68–82.

5. Krutak, *Tattoo Traditions of Asia*, 6.

Ultimately, who started tattooing for spiritual reasons—and when—is irrelevant. Tattooing is global. Archaeological evidence for tattooing in the United States goes back to 1600 BCE, maybe as far back as 3500 BCE.[6] A mummy with a mustache-like tattoo, recovered in Chile, is estimated to date back to 2500 BCE.[7] Indigenous peoples in Papua New Guinea in Southeast Asia have tattooed since at least 1650 BCE according to carbon dating of tattooing implements.[8] Almost anywhere you go, at one point there were people who tattooed. This is a universal phenomenon we can all embrace.

Tattoos and Magick More Recently

There are myriad spiritual tattooing traditions practiced today or in the relatively recent past. I have organized a sampling of them. Again, the purpose of this book is what *you* can do with your tattoos. Many of these practices belong to groups of people I am not a part of, and many of you aren't either. I can't tell you it is okay to take these practices for your own. I only want to give you enough information to understand that the use of tattoos for spiritual reasons is perfectly valid. The actual execution will be discussed later on in the context of the Witchcraft system that I, and many of you, practice.

Tattooing for Help During the Afterlife

Death and what comes after was and is a big deal to many peoples, going back hundreds of thousands of years. Funeral rituals are truly a global phenomenon, just like tattooing. It should come as no surprise that tattoos in many cultures were at least partly designed to assist with the afterlife.

---

6. Deter-Wolf et al., "Ancient Native American Bone Tattooing Tools and Pigments."

7. Deter-Wolf et al., "The World's Oldest Tattoos."

8. Furey, "Archaeological Evidence for Tattooing in Polynesia and Micronesia," 160.

Tattoos have been given to people so they can be identified in the afterlife. This is the case for the Naga people in Myanmar, the Adi people in Tibet, and the Kondh people in India.[9] There were physical items that could be used for identification—necklaces for the Naga and brass for the Adi—but if you couldn't afford them, tattoos were the way to go.[10] This is practiced by relatively few people today, but its spiritual importance cannot be understated.

Sometimes, tattoos determined what you did during the afterlife. Fully tattooed women of the Long Glat in Borneo could bathe in the streams of the afterlife and catch pearls. Partially tattooed women could only sit and watch, and women who weren't tattooed couldn't go anywhere near the stream.[11] For Tharu and Newari in Tibet, women's tattoos would include household items that one would want or need to have in the afterlife.[12] In other words, if you didn't get a tattoo of the item, you wouldn't be able to use it after death. The Dawan in Indonesia used their tattoos as a currency of sorts. After death, the Dawan barter their tattoos for fire to light their way to their ancestors.[13]

Finally, tattoos helped people reach the afterlife. The Lakota believed that when a warrior died, their tattoos would be inspected on their way to the afterlife by a being named the Owl-Maker. If they did not have the appropriate tattoos, they would be turned into ghostly wanderers instead.[14] For the Dayak in Indonesia, tattoos reflect the individual's experiences and deeds throughout their

9. Siegel, "India on the Road."

10. Hambly, *The History of Tattooing*, 52–53.

11. Sanders and Vail, *Customizing the Body*, 11.

12. "Tattoo Tourism."

13. Krutak, *Indigenous Tattoo Traditions*, chapter 6.

14. Jennings, *100 Places to See After You Die*, 15.

life. This makes them truly an identifier of that person and their unique life. When they die, they face inspection by the guardian of the bridge over the River of Death. If their tattoos did not indicate their success in life, they were eaten by a catfish spirit. If they had the right tattoos, they went on to a place of darkness where their tattoos emitted a golden light, illuminating the rest of the way.[15]

Tattoo Protection Talismans

In some cultures, tattoos were given to provide protection. The Amazigh peoples in Tunisia have tattoo designs that hold the power to protect against malevolent spirits and aid in healing.[16] An old practice among the Pashtun in Iran, Afghanistan, and Pakistan is to make tattoos for people to avoid the evil eye. The tattoo is named "sheen khaal" for the blue/green dots that make it up.[17] For Ainu women in Japan, getting tattoos protected against demons, which they believed to cause disease.[18] The tattoos allowed them to be mistaken for goddesses, making the demons too afraid to bother them.[19] People in Thailand have specific magickal tattoos known as Sak Yant, which can provide protection among many other things. In fact, it is said that people with a Sak Yant protection tattoo will be impervious to bullets.[20] Similarly, the Naga in Myanmar have tattoos believed to protect the wearer from knife and machete cuts.[21]

---

15. Krutak, "In the Realm of Spirits."

16. Krutak, *Indigenous Tattoo Traditions*, chapter 1.

17. Griswold, *I Am the Beggar of the World*, 14.

18. Ankirskiy, "Perception of Tattoos," 11.

19. Jang, "World Cultures."

20. Cook, "Tattoos, Corporeality and the Self," 24.

21. Krutak, "Naga Tattoos of Myanmar."

Magickal Medicine

Medicinal tattoos, as a form of sympathetic magick, are quite widespread. Europe's oldest intact human mummy had sixty-one tattoos, which were frequently located above arthritic joints. This led some academics to believe the tattoos were meant to be medicinal.[22] Remember also the body found in Russia with the snake tattoo over the broken bone. The snake in that area was believed to have healing powers, so tattooing the snake over the broken bone might have been a way for the bone to receive the restorative power of the snake. Indigenous Alaskans would tattoo over joints to prevent disease-causing spirits from entering the body.[23] While the ancient traditions of the Kalinga in the Philippines have all but died out, we do know people could receive tattoos on their neck as a cure for goiter.[24] The Wodaabe in West Africa use tattooing for pain relief.[25] The Ainu in Japan would tattoo to restore eyesight.[26] Finally, the Kayan in Borneo would tattoo a bead design on the wrists to prevent the loss of one's soul, which they believed caused disease.[27] It was believed sickness was the result of the soul leaving the body, and the bead was supposed to tie the soul down to, or rather into, the body.

Adopting Animal and Spirit Abilities

While not as common, there are magickal tattoos that allow someone to take on the abilities of a particular animal. The Meriam peoples of the Torres Strait Islands had many such possible totems. For

---

22. Krutak, *Spiritual Skin,* 144–46.

23. Krutak, "Therapeutic Tattooing in the Arctic," 107.

24. Abbacan-Tuguic and Marnag, "Whatok (Tattooe)," 738.

25. Krutak, *Indigenous Tattoo Traditions,* chapter 1.

26. Krutak, *Tattoo Traditions of Asia,* 25.

27. Krutak, *Spiritual Skin,* 140.

example, people who had cassowary tattoos could run faster. In New Georgia, the largest island in the Solomon Islands, the totem tattoo has to go on specific body parts. Getting a porpoise tattoo won't mean much there unless you get it on your legs. If you do, the tattoo will give you speed for swimming. In Myanmar, tattooing a tiger made one more cunning.[28] Men of the Mentawai in Indonesia will get small dog paw tattoos on their inner thighs and the tops of their feet to allow them to run as fast as a dog.[29] In Vancouver among the Haida, a halibut tattoo might prevent the wearer from drowning.[30] Some totemic abilities came not from the tattoo design but the tattoo material. Among the Kwengo in Namibia, deer fat rubbed into a fresh tattoo provided speed and endurance.[31] The Nlaka'pamux in Canada had a practice not dissimilar, where tattooing one's guardian spirit allowed the individual to take on their powers. Getting a tattoo of a mountain guardian spirit made you strong; a tattoo of an arrow spirit made you more skilled at archery.[32]

While not linked to an animal, ship parts were tattooed on some American sailors in the beginning of the twentieth century, functioning as a form of sympathetic magick. Eyes were tattooed on eyelids or nipples to increase watchfulness. Propellers were tattooed on the butt to enable someone to move more dexterously and quickly. Hinges were placed on the joints for strength.[33]

---

28. Lippert, "Tattooing," 164.

29. Krutak, *Indigenous Tattoo Traditions*, chapter 6.

30. Bunn-Marcuse, "Wearing Identity," 44.

31. Krutak, *Indigenous Tattoo Traditions*, chapter 1.

32. Krutak, *Spiritual Skin*, 70.

33. Lippert, "Tattooing," 164.

Channeling Children

Tattoos are frequently linked with courtship and reproduction too. The Wodaabe of West and Central Africa tattoo for fertility and to magickally increase beauty.[34] Tattoos in the genital area are given to Makonde women in Tanzania and Mozambique. These are supposed to get them a husband and enhance fertility. The Siberian Chukchi will cast fertility spells with tattoos specifically on the cheeks.[35]

Other Magickal Uses

There is a grab bag of other magickal uses for tattoos, which I am adding last to round things out. Chukchi warriors in Siberia would tattoo representations of men they had just killed on their bodies to capture their opponents' souls and turn them into spiritual helpers. Thai tattoo masters had the ability to create tattoos to make people act in an awestruck manner to the wearer. The Mentawai in Indonesia have tattoo designs of beads on the backs of their hands, created to make the hands more dexterous.[36] Several tribes in Africa, including the Sekele Bushmen in Southern Angola, the Kwengo of Namibia, and the Wodaabe, have tattoos to bring good luck.[37] The Thai Sak Yant tattoos I mentioned previously are frequently given for protection, yes, but in truth they are pretty much all-purpose. You can get a Sak Yant tattoo for almost anything, from good luck and wealth to power and charisma.[38] Tattoo artists in Polynesia were able to control and manipulate mana, or spiritual power, in their clients through tattooing.[39]

---

34. Krutak, *Indigenous Tattoo Traditions,* chapter 1.

35. Krutak, *Spiritual Skin,* 138.

36. Krutak, *Spiritual Skin,* 140.

37. Krutak, *Indigenous Tattoo Traditions,* chapter 1.

38. "Sak Yant Information."

39. Krutak, "Embodied Symbols of the South Seas."

I have been mentioning peoples in Asia and Africa a lot, but even if you identify as European, you have documented talismanic tattooing in your history. In 1609, an Englishman named Simon Forman tattooed the signs of Venus, Jupiter, and Cancer on himself. These entities governed his horoscope, so he believed by getting them tattooed on himself he could harness the power of his horoscope and thereby alter the trajectory of his life. This mirrored a tradition in the area of drawing symbols on the body to achieve magickal results.[40] To be fair, though, those were not strictly meant to be permanent.

The Sanctity of Tattooing

Tattoos aren't just magickal for the benefits they can give. The application of tattoos itself is sacred. You can see that first and foremost through the impact the tattoo ritual has on people's lives. Naga women in Myanmar are tattooed around the age of puberty. Now that they are able to bear children, they are suitable for marriage. Interestingly, among the Naga little attention is paid to a woman's first menses as the sign that she is able to bear children and be marriable. Instead, it is determined largely by whether she has gone through the puberty rites of tattooing.[41] Now, of course, the tattooing isn't necessary for someone to bear children. Many people without tattoos have children. It is a sign, though, of how sacred the act of tattooing is that it should accompany such a momentous occasion and symbolically be assigned this power. The Naga are not the only ones with these kinds of magickal initiatory traditions. Tattooing accompanies initiations for other peoples, such as the Kayabi in Brazil. The Kayabi change their names frequently to mark significant life moments, new achievements, and so on. Those names are often divined by a shaman, making them quite sacred, and are frequently

40. Rosecrans, "Wearing the Universe," 47–48.

41. Longchar, "Rites of Passage," 37.

tattooed onto their bodies. At the very least, a Kayabi man will always have a tattoo of the name provided when he, as a boy, was initiated into a full-fledged member of their society.[42]

You can tell that the act of tattooing is sacred in many places by what type of person does the tattooing. For the Paiwan in Taiwan, tattooing used to be performed by a shaman.[43] For the Marquesans in Fiji, the tattoo artist isn't necessarily a priest, but he might as well be one. His relationship with his patron deity is so strong that the power from his deity envelops a person as they are being tattooed.[44] Sak Yant, the magickal tattooing system from Thailand, is traditionally applied by a Buddhist monk, though it isn't a hard rule. Among the Kayabi in Brazil, some, but not all, tattoos are designed through a shaman. The shaman's spiritual helpers choose the design, which the shaman must divine through conversations with them.[45]

Finally, frequently, there are elements of tattooing rituals that are or were explicitly spiritual in nature. This is particularly so for the practices people used to have on the Marshall Islands in the Pacific Ocean. On the Marshall Islands, the gods were summoned before a tattoo was given to determine whether they believed it was a good idea. If it was good, offerings were made to the gods of tattooing. Prayers and blessings were said over the person to be tattooed. Following that, there was a ceremony of chanting and ritualistic drumming.[46] Among the Marquesans, the process of collecting the pigment for the ink was highly labor intensive and spiritualized. It was very dangerous, spiritually speaking. If done incorrectly, the per-

---

42. Krutak, *Indigenous Tattoo Traditions,* chapter 3.

43. Krutak, "Losing Your Head Among the Tattooed Headhunters of Taiwan."

44. Krutak, *Indigenous Tattoo Traditions,* chapter 4.

45. Krutak, *Spiritual Skin,* 84.

46. Kaeppler, "Tattooed Beauty," 12.

son preparing the pigment could be infested with negative energy. The kernels of the candlenut were placed into a fire and the smoke funneled up to a smooth stone, which was constantly and continually tapped while the soot collected on it. When the tattoo artist arrived, the soot would be mixed with water. All of this took place within a sacred house built specifically for the tattoo, which was burned to the ground when the tattoo was done.[47] Sak Yant are applied in an explicitly spiritual ceremony. Offerings are made, frequently flowers and incense. Tools are blessed. Prayers are chanted by the monk to imbue the tattoo with energy, and a gold leaf talisman is applied afterward for blessings.[48]

* · · · *

If your ancestors came from Europe, it may feel a little disappointing to hear so little discussion about European magickal tattooing. I'm not saying one man in the seventeenth century is the extent of magickal tattoo practices in Europe. There are ancient European tattooing practices people hypothesize to be magickal, such as the snake tattoo found in Russia. We can't say for sure, though, because there is no written record of what they were for. And most cultures on this planet did not keep meticulous records. It seems like much of magickal tattooing is confined to Africa and Southeast Asia, but that's just because those places have magickal traditions that exist today.

If you want more exposition about tattoos and spiritual traditions, I suggest the books at the end of the chapter. In particular, I highly recommend anything by Lars Krutak. He is a well-known and respected scholar on tattooing who makes a point of connecting respectfully with the peoples of Indigenous tattooing cultures. He

---

47. Handy, *Tattooing in the Marquesas*, 10.

48. Jerrentrup, "The Body, the Spirit, and the Other," 38.

publishes books and has a vast blog with more information than you could want.

What this chapter has meant to show is how universal tattoos are for magick. Tattoo magick is something that can readily be used in any system. It just falls on us to figure out how to create it in the system we are a part of. I practice, as many of us do, in the system of magick or "Witchcraft," which derived from Western ceremonial magick, folk magick, and Neopaganism, and I will start to show you how to work tattoo magick in that system in the next chapter.

Some Further Reading

Written on the Body: The Tattoo in European and American History, edited by Jane Caplan[49]

Indigenous Tattoo Traditions: A History of Humanity Through Skin and Ink by Lars Krutak

Spiritual Tattoo: A Cultural History of Tattooing, Piercing, Scarification, Branding, and Implants by John A. Rush

---

49. *Written on the Body* has little in the way of discussing magick. The chapter on Simon Forman is mostly the extent of the magickal discourse. It is a nice book on European and American tattooing history, though.

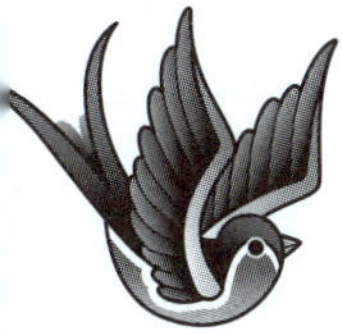

2
The Ways Healed Tattoos Can Be Used in Magick

In my opinion, there are three primary reasons tattoos are powerful magickal tools. Some or all of them will apply to you and your tattoo. First, tattoos are rather potent symbols. Symbols, as props to focus the mind on one's intention during spellwork, are an indispensable part of magick. Let's face it: A motivation spell with a light blue candle feels very different from a motivation spell with a red candle. Now, the effectiveness of a symbol depends on how easily your mind can make the association between the symbol and what it represents. What makes tattoos so special is the fact that you are around yours all the time—definitely more than the yellow candle in your magickal cabinet or the sigil you made five minutes ago. Any association you make will be reinforced and strengthened the more often it's made. You see your tattoo, with few exceptions, all the time. The more often you look at the tattoo you got to be more self-confident, the more often you'll think, "I got that to remind myself to be more self-confident" or "Wow, this really is a good reminder to be self-confident." You don't even need to be consciously aware of the association. Your brain will make the connection subconsciously, and it will be strengthened subconsciously every time you see the tattoo.

The second reason tattoos are so powerful is how connected they are to you. Whenever you see that self-confidence tattoo, yes, you think, "This is for self-confidence," but you also think, "This is my tattoo. This is mine." And again, with some exceptions, we see our tattoos a lot. Far more than, again, that yellow candle or brand-new sigil. Also, really, how much more connected can you get than to something that is literally inside you? Now, the reason this is important is because we resonate with things we are connected to. We like them more. And as I'm sure most of you know, doing your preferred type of magick feels very different from one you never got into. It feels more powerful. It feels more right. And yes, it really *is* more powerful; interacting with things we are connected to improves how well we work with them in a lot of different ways.[50] We remember them better, notice them better, work with them more innovatively, and develop higher quality outputs with them. Academics haven't seen yet whether Witchcraft is one of those outputs, nor will they anytime soon. But it is possible that we work better magick with our tattoos because of how connected we are with them. And if you think back to the spells you vibe with most, you'll feel how true that is.

Finally, your tattoo is powerful because it is a piece of you—both literally and figuratively. This is powerful first and foremost because, as it is a piece of you, it can be a stand-in for you, much like your signature is a representation of you. Magick works best when there is something to represent the recipient of the spell. That's why we frequently get a lock of hair, picture, birthdate, or name to use in spellwork. There are a myriad of ways you can do fun magickal tricks

---

50. Atatsi et al., "Predicting Task Performance from Psychological Ownership and Innovative Work Behaviour," 1; Englert, "What Is 'Mere' About the Mere Ownership Effect?" 75, 93; Cunningham et al., "Yours or Mine?" 312.

with that on its own. But what makes the tattoo especially powerful, if you are performing spellwork for yourself, is that it is both the representation and the symbol. When you decide you want to use your tattoo for a spell for you specifically, focusing on the tattoo provides the ability to be laser-focused simultaneously on the intention and the recipient in a way almost no other magick I know of can. It is an extremely powerful way to channel your intention directly to you.

The practices that I share in this chapter, the ways you can use your tattoo in magick, are derived from these three reasons. You will also see some of this in the chapters coming up on devotional tattoos and ancestor worship tattoos.

Batteries of Magickal Energy

Your body is humming with energy. From the sodium ions that make way for your neurons to communicate with each other, to your aura, all parts of your body produce some amount of energy. Even the parts of your body that are tattooed are humming with energy. And your tattoo, again, is a meaningful symbol. It narrows your attention to a specific concept or idea when you see it. That attention, over time, affects the energies residing in the tattoo to reflect that concept. You can call upon that energy wherever you are, whenever you need it, if your intention matches that symbolism.

To be fair, this effect is stronger under the following circumstances. First, the tattoo is explicitly meaningful to you, and you know what the meaning is. In this case, your brain will be more focused whenever you see it, charging it better. Second, you have been consciously feeding it with energy. Third, you like the tattoo. If you hate it, you are channeling negative thoughts toward it, which interferes with its ability to be used for something positive. If none of these three are true now, that doesn't mean you should lose hope. In fact, by finding a new, purposeful use for your tattoo—magick—you can begin to like it again.

So, work with it—in inconsequential ways for now, to be safe—to build a better connection and feel better about it. In the meantime, I have some suggestions for those other two circumstances.

Exercise: Finding the Meaning in Your Tattoo

As I mentioned, it is certainly easier to use your tattoo for magick if that tattoo means something specific. That focuses your attention, intention, and energies when you look at the tattoo, which primes it for magick. What happens if you got it just because you wanted to, though? Or just because it looks cool?

People make associations with everything. Just ask your high school English teacher, your therapist, or the person who always reads way too much into the things you say. The associations don't need to be conscious, either, so there likely is one association or more you have developed subconsciously. Maybe that was why you picked the tattoo in the first place. An association or associations could also develop over time. The developed association doesn't have to be conscious and honestly likely won't be. Either way, if you can't think of a meaning, you will want to probe your subconscious to get a better sense of what associations you have with your tattoo. That's what this exercise is for.

I want you to pull out a piece of paper and a pen. Using your phone might also work, but I find this goes a lot better when physically writing. Set a timer for three minutes, then start writing. Begin with "my [insert short description of tattoo] tattoo means" and just keep going. Do not stop. When the three minutes are up, take a look at what you wrote. All of these words point to meanings and associations you have with your tattoo.

This is a book on Witchcraft, and I assume you're reading this to figure out what magick you can work with your tattoo. Therefore, if you haven't already, I want you to look for themes. Find the commonalities in words or meanings and see if any of them mirror an intention. If you used words like "strong," "hardcore," and "shield," then protection might be an intention associated with your tattoo. If you wrote things like "sunshine," "grass is green," and "joy," the intention might be positivity. "Gold," "security," and "productive" might point to a focus on prosperity. "Life," "wholeness," and "nurse" might be a health intention.

This exercise is meant to help you get to your subconscious mind. The conscious, thinking, analyzing, second-guessing mind is supposed to take a back seat. To prevent your conscious mind from interfering, I have a few tips.

My first tip is to write whatever is the first thing to come to mind. Seriously, first thing. Do not second-guess yourself. If you think to yourself "that's a stupid thought," say "fuck you" to that voice in your head and write it anyway! If this is something that your subconscious backpedals after writing it, you'll likely see the next few words are "no, actually" or something similar. But don't doubt yourself. If you consciously think "no, that's definitely wrong; I don't think that," keep going with it. We all know that how we subconsciously feel can contradict what we think we believe. And magick speaks to the subconscious.

The second tip is to not let the stubborn, obsessive, perfectionist part of you take over. Is your handwriting getting sloppy? Keep writing. Is it veering off or getting larger and larger until it goes over another line of text? Keep writing. Do you think you spelled something wrong? Keep writing. All of this would be natural. You're not going slowly enough to think about spelling. For those who have obsessively pristine handwriting, you aren't going slowly enough to make sure everything is nice and neat. It's okay. I won't judge.

The final tip is to not allow yourself to stop writing. When you stop writing, the conscious mind comes in and starts thinking about what you should write next. If you find you don't know what you are going to write next, the trick is to start writing the last word over and over and over. Say the word in your head, too, to drown out any conscious thoughts that are bubbling up. At a certain point, something will click, and you'll begin to write again.

You'll find that this is great as an exercise for interpreting symbols in divination. Did you see something while scrying an obsidian sphere? Do the exercise with "[Symbol] in the obsidian sphere means ..." Do you keep seeing something that you think might be a sign? "The [thing you saw] is a sign that ..." Have a tarot reading where you are absolutely not sure about a specific card? Write the question on top, if desired the cards pulled with the one you are asking about circled, and "[Name of card] in this reading means ..." You can also use the exercise to plan out a spell or figure out ingredients when you are a little stuck.

Ritual for Consciously Charging Your Tattoo with Magickal Energy

Consciously charging your tattoo with magickal energy is more or less the same as casting a spell, but rather than send the energy out into the ether, you bring all the energy inside you, directly toward the tattoo. Below is a short ritual. Before you start, figure out a visualization that will correspond to the energies you want to instill in your tattoo. Don't make it too complicated because you'll be doing multiple things at once. You'll also want to read through the ritual before beginning, as you'll be asked to close your eyes.

Sit down to meditate. Close your eyes. Take a few minutes to breathe and focus your concentration on just the rise and fall of your stomach. If your mind wanders, bring your attention back to your stomach without judgment. When you feel sufficiently relaxed, I want you to imagine you are like a tree with roots that sink into and connect with everything they grow in, pulling in spiritual nourishment. Feel your spiritual, energetic roots grow out of your spine, reaching downward until they hit the earth. The roots spread out, growing in all directions in the soil. The more they grow, the more you feel connected to Nature. After a minute, or when you feel it is enough, stop growing your roots.

Bring your chosen visualization to mind. Focus on it intensely. Imagine expanding the visualization until it envelops your body. It sinks into you. It becomes you. You are a vessel for that intention. Anything that enters you will be infused with you and therefore infused with your intention. Now, take a deep breath in, visualizing energies from the earth rising through the roots and filling you. Inhale again, drawing up more energy. Repeat. With every breath, you draw in more and more. As the energy enters your body, feel it change, charged with your intention. Bring in more until you feel you can contain nothing else in you. See and feel the energy coursing throughout your body, infused with your intention.

Now, when you breathe in, you are no longer going to take in energy from Nature. Instead, imagine all of this energy being pulled inward toward a spot at the center of your chest where your lungs are. The energy that was moving all over you now swirls between your kneecaps and your nose. The energy feels stronger as it becomes more concentrated. Your body vibrates ever so slightly, a low hum of magickal potential. Breathe in again, and the energy is compressed from your neck to your navel. Your body vibrates more, a strong tingle. Breathe in one more time, and the energy gets pulled all the way to the spot in your heart/lung area.

At this point, your entire body feels like it is pulsing with energy. The energy is almost overwhelming, hyperconcentrated within you.

Breathe in deeply, and on an exhale, send that ball of energy up your windpipe and out of your mouth. Allow it to float serenely eight inches in front of your face. With the intention in your mind, grab the sphere of energy with your hand and smack it into your tattoo. In a shower of magickal sparks, your tattoo tingles, and then the energy dissipates.

Retract your energetic roots from the earth, bringing them back up until they have fully merged with you. Do this ritual as many times as you want, however often you want to charge the tattoo.

...

If you are feeling overwhelmed at all after this practice, don't panic. That can happen when you bring up that much energy. Get on your knees and tilt forward, like you are bowing, until your forehead touches the floor. Allow the energy that is still in your body to flow out of your head toward the earth. Breathe slowly.

As an alternative, you could breathe the energies into a magickal oil that you apply to your tattoo regularly. You can even put the oil into a scrub to exfoliate your tattoo while you shower. That way you're indulging in magick *and* self-care. To make a salt scrub, pour one cup coarse sea salt in a jar, then pour in a quarter cup jojoba or coconut oil and stir until the salt is evenly coated. Add desired herbs or essential oils. If using essential oils, use no more than twenty drops, and please be careful. Many essential oils, such as the citruses and cinnamon, can be *very* painful on the skin. Also avoid using peppermint oil because the cold sensation can be very intense, especially in more sensitive areas.

Activating Your Tattoo's Energies

So, your tattoo is charged, right? How do you use it? Do the energies just sit there in your body? If you want them to, they can. If there is a physical intention, by proximity the energies might start to do their work. That is not the fastest or most efficient way, though. It is best to stimulate the inert energies and then guide them to do their work, just as in any spell.

I use touch to activate my tattoos. With a fingernail, trace your tattoo. Trace it repeatedly and consistently while you chant. The chant should not be generic but tailored to your intention. If you want, in addition to the chant, you can visualize. This technique has the advantage that as you are stimulating the energies in the tattoo, you're also stimulating your skin. You can use the physical sensation to concentrate better on what you are trying to do.

It works best if the tracing pattern is simpler so you don't have to concentrate a lot on it and can get into a trance better. Don't feel disappointed if the particular tattoo you want to use for magick is rather complicated. That doesn't have to be an issue. Is there a small part of the tattoo that is the focus or most meaningful part? Perhaps the sword that the Valkyrie riding the panther is holding to the sky? Or the ball of flame the giant dragon is spitting? Or the head of the laughing skeleton on the motorcycle? If you can't think of or see one, you can always just trace a circle around the tattoo.

The beauty of activating your tattoo is that since the tattoo is already charged with energy, you don't really need to activate it within ritual. It's like a sachet or talisman you carry with you, meaning it works quite well for intentions you might have while away from home.

Using Your Tattoo as Symbolism for Spellwork

As I mentioned at the beginning of this chapter, symbols are incredibly useful in magick to help focus the mind on the intention. Tattoos are symbols. Therefore, you can use tattoos the way you would any symbolism in your spells.

You can use your tattoo as the centerpiece in spells. Use it any way you would use a sigil. Draw it on a piece of paper and put it in a sachet, carve it in a candle and burn it, trace it into the sand and let the waves wash it away. Your tattoo would be great as a meditative piece, if you like to work ritual through meditative trance. If you print it out, it's great with markers as a coloring spell. I recognize we don't all have printers, but you can take a picture with your phone, isolate the tattoo pretty easily with free editing software, and take it to your local copy center where they allow you to print things out. If you want, you can layer on symbolism. Sprinkle a corresponding herb into the shape of your tattoo on your altar. If you are drawing it, use a marker that is in a color corresponding to your intention. You can use symbolism that corresponds to the tattoo itself, provided you don't find that distracting and it immediately makes you think of your tattoo. If you have a panther tattoo, while you're working with it, play jungle sounds with panther calls. If it is a rose tattoo, burn rose incense or anoint yourself with rose oil.

Symbolism is frequently used in spellwork even when it isn't a central part. It works really well at setting the atmosphere or keeping the mind focused on the intention by surrounding yourself with reminders of it. Imagine a ritual for peace that includes taking a blue bag and putting in a piece of paper you wrote *peace* on. Now imagine a ritual where you have the same blue bag and piece of paper but there are several white and light blue candles burning around them. The candles are each sitting on top of a peace sign. You are wearing a light blue, comfortable outfit. Chamomile incense smolders, and a ring of lavender circles the blue bag. Which example feels more like "peace" to you? Do you think you'll keep "peace" in your mind more easily with one of these? There is nothing saying you can't use your tattoo to bolster the primary symbolism by having it in your line of sight, especially if there is another type of magick you want to do.

Print it out and put it on the walls or in front of your candles or poppet. If you don't want to print it out, position a mirror behind your altar so your tattoo is visible while you work. If the tattoo represents magick or your magickal power, carve it into your altar. Provided the association between your tattoo and your intention is strong enough, you can meditate upon it prior to starting your spell to get you into the right mindset.

Personal Sign

I mentioned tattoos being a representation for you, much like the lock of hair, drop of blood, or birthdate we use to identify someone in a spell. It makes sense if you think about it; tattoos are a part of you, literally. And many of us have tattoos that are either so dear to us or so identified with us that they become a signifier for us. A personal sign, if you will. My partner's brother has a sleeve tattoo that's themed after a specific TV, video, and card game franchise we all know and love from our childhood. It looks absolutely sick. When I think of him, the first thing I think of is not his face. It's not the band he's a part of. It's not the place where he bartends (he makes a mean margarita, by the way). It's his tattoo. That is what I think of first. His tattoo is him, to me. It is his personal sign.

So, what's the point? Why should you care to use your tattoo this way? To start, it's a representation that is much more easily mystical. When you write your legal name, does that feel powerful? No. It's mundane, tied to your non-magickal life. You use it too much in everyday occurrences for it to seem like a special and powerful version of you. That's why using a lock of your hair or a safely extracted drop of your blood feels so much more authentically magickal. But let's face it: Some of us are needlephobic or queasy at the sight of blood. And some of us are bald or have shaved heads. So, what's a Witch to do? Draw your tattoo! You aren't using it in everyday life.

You aren't putting it on official documents or in an email signature, so your tattoo doesn't have these connections. Using it in spellwork often enough draws a connection to mysticism that is not competing with your "boring" aspects—not to mention the connection is more symbolic, and your subconscious, intuitive self thinks more in symbols. Your tattoo can be, therefore, a much more mystical signifier, making it more powerful in magick.

The second reason is what your tattoo symbolizes: an idealized part of you. I have always associated my triangle tattoo with myself. And at some point, if not at the very beginning, I associated the tattoo with strength. So, my tattoo is me, and is strength. Tattoo = me + strength = strong me. I realized that my tattoo reflects and signifies a specific part of me, an aspect of myself that even if it is hidden, or rarely comes out, is accessible. Using my tattoo as a personal identifier provides a path for me to channel and embody Strong Me. By using that tattoo as my identifier, I have become "Strong Jake."

If you want to bring out Ideal You quickly and temporarily, you can use the tattoo for aspecting or glamours. Trace the tattoo with your nail and feel the tingling of the skin. Chant: "This is me, three times three, so mote it be." Visualize the tattoo glowing, brighter and brighter. The Idealized You is getting stronger, waking up. When you feel the energy is peaking, stop outlining and smack your hand on the tattoo like you're hitting a computer to make it work. Like a stone dropping in water, the moment your hand hits the tattoo, the energy is released throughout your body. See it. As the energy passes over each part of your body, it changes. Your posture changes. The way you hold yourself changes. Even your thoughts are transformed, though you still have control over your body. Everything the energy touches becomes Idealized You. In a split second, the energy reaches your head and the transformation is complete.

Glamours can weaken over time, sometimes quite rapidly. For me, that is fine; I only activate Super Strong Me when I'm about to be in a very unpleasant situation, which usually ends pretty quickly. When I am finished, I dismiss the glamour by looking in the mirror. I imagine the pulsing aura of energy that is my glamour, look myself in the eyes, and say quite genuinely, "Thank you. Thank you. Thank you. Thank you." And with a long exhale, I visualize the aura fading. My posture becomes normal. My thoughts become normal.

You might want this change to be temporary because you don't always need to have those characteristics. You also might have multiple versions of yourself that you could want to aspect. So, you could use different tattoos for them. If you want to bring out Ideal You permanently, I would perform a more involved ritual or spell. Channel more energy into it. And keep in mind that true, lasting change, unlike a glamour, is gradual.

A Tattoo Spell to Become Your Ideal Self

This spell uses mud to help you become your Ideal Self. For those of you who are curious, mud was chosen because it draws out toxins. Therefore, it will draw out what you do not want to be while the energies from your tattoo infuse what is left with your ideal characteristics. Put the mixture on your skin, and after some time, wipe it off to reveal your Ideal Self! As a note of caution, this spell will require you to carve your tattoo into a candle. I recognize many of us have tattoos that make this particularly difficult to do. I have an exercise later in this chapter with a tip on how to work around that.

> ***Warning:*** *This spell can get a little messy. If you only have a shower and no bathtub, apply the mud to yourself on the bathroom floor and be very careful about slipping.*

Ingredients

Herbs that corresponds to the quality you are trying to embody, about three ounces[51]

Plastic wrap

A couple pounds of mud[52]

A pot or large bowl

A needle or pin for carving

A long spoon

Six taper candles in a color or colors corresponding to that quality; use pillar candles if it's a large tattoo

Candleholders

Lighter or matches

Spell

A day before you start the ritual, spread some of the herbs on top of a piece of plastic wrap. The piece should be large enough to cover your tattoo and then some. Then, very carefully apply the wrap to your tattoo. Go around the area a few times to secure the wrap. The herbs should be on top of the tattoo. As you are wrapping yourself, repeat:

[Quality you want] *I will be.*

After you finish the wrapping, go about your day.

The next day, place the mud into the pot or large bowl. Put it on a flat surface. Pour the remainder of the herbs around the bowl in a circle.

---

51. Rub some of the herbs on your skin for about thirty seconds to make sure they don't irritate it, because they're going to be on for a while.

52. You can buy some online.

Carve your tattoo into each candle; on the opposite side of the candle, carve: "This is me, three times three, so mote it be." If you want it shorter, carve: "TIM3x3SMIB." Empower the candles for the quality your tattoo embodies, which you are bringing out of you. Secure the candles in their holders, and place a candle at all four corners of your bathtub and light them. Place the remaining two behind and to the sides of the bowl and light them.

Very carefully remove the plastic wrap from your tattoo so you don't spill the herbs. When you look at the herbs, notice they are slightly pulsing light. That is the energy of your Ideal Self. Carefully transfer the herbs to the pot or bowl with the mud, all the while seeing the glow. Start stirring clockwise with the spoon. As you stir, the glow permeates into the mud. Start to chant:

That is me,
[Quality] *is me,*
Three times three,
So mote it be.

The chant is not to raise energy; it's to help set the intention into the mud. So, chant and stir until it seems like the herbs have been well combined into the mud.

Take your clothes off and get into the bathtub. Apply the mud to your body, to as much of yourself as possible. Start with your face. As you cover yourself in the mud, conjure up a visualization of yourself embodying the characteristic you're bringing into yourself and start raising energy with the following chant:

This is me,[53]
Three times three,
So mote it be.

---

53. Note that it says "this," while the last chant said "that."

Continue chanting until your energy has reached its peak, then send it off. Finish applying the mud and lie in the bathtub. If your preferred method of raising energy involves your hands, perhaps using a rattle, raise energy after you've finished applying the mud.

Spend nine minutes with the mud on you. Try to think only positive thoughts, but feel free to let your mind wander. If you want, you can visualize scenes where you're demonstrating the quality you've brought out in yourself, but it's not necessary. After nine minutes, wash the mud off your body. As you do so, chant:

Now I'm me,
[Quality] *is me,*
Three times three,
So mote it be.

A Magickal Microcosm

We've all heard of voodoo dolls. A voodoo doll works because the doll is a representation of a person. What happens to it happens to the whole person. Similarly, since a tattoo can be a stand-in for you, what you do to your tattoo you do to all of you. Can't get incense in every crack and crevice for a purification? Bathe the tattoo in incense instead. Have a full-body sunburn but can't afford to bathe in the right healing oils? Apply a small amount with intention to your tattoo.

You can also draw on the tattoo or the skin around it. If this tattoo is a representation of you, changing the tattoo can start the magickal process of making changes in you. Do you need to calm down? Take a blue marker and mindfully color the tattoo blue.[54] Is there an open space inside the tattoo, even if small? In an eye, maybe?

---

54. Trust me: It will work. I tested it on my blackout sleeve. If I can see blue on my blackout sleeve, you can see it on your tattoo.

Draw a tiny representation of the outcome within to show your outcome already within you. On the flipside, draw a basic shape around the tattoo to show you are surrounded by or in contact with the quality you desire. For example, you could draw a heart for a lover, maybe with a small list of the traits you are looking for within the heart.

Draw a sigil and connect it to the tattoo, maybe with an arrow to show it coming to you. Or you could even make a sigil *with* a tattoo. Say you want to bring prosperity to you, and you have a tattoo with your birth date in Roman numerals. More likely than not there's an *X* somewhere in there. Draw a line down the middle of the *X*, and then make an upward diagonal as seen in the picture below. Congratulations! Within the *X*, you just made a bindrune with Gebo, Isa, and Fehu for prosperity.

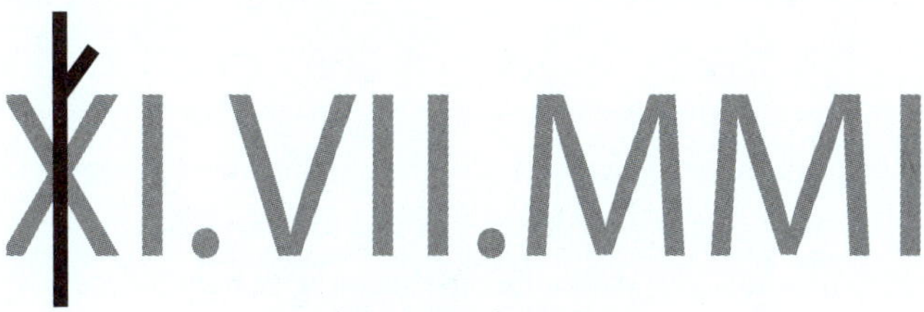

Birth Date Bindrune Tattoo

Divination

Note: *I will caution you ahead of time that these tattoos are best on your forearms or front or side thigh, because you have to be able to see it in detail without straining. If you can't do that, put it somewhere you can see easily in a mirror without any muscle strain.*

For people who are not familiar with the term, "scrying" is usually defined as a method of divination involving staring into a reflective object. The usual tool for scrying is a crystal ball or blackened mirror. When you stare into one of those just right, any of the following—or more—could happen: You see clouds that move in a particular direction or pattern; you receive impressions or emotions; you see images in the surface; you see images in your mind; you see entire scenes play out. If you receive an impression or message, it can relate to a number of things. These include reminders, potential future paths, what to avoid, what to seek, and other inspiration for problem-solving. If you receive an image, you would analyze it like you would a symbol in a dream or tea leaf reading. You can call scrying a form of psychism or your subconscious/Higher Self/Divinity using a blank canvas to communicate information to you. The two aren't mutually exclusive!

When most people say "scrying," they are referring to staring at reflective surfaces only. I have always felt that idea to be so limiting. Truthfully, you can scry absolutely anything. You might not see scenes when you scry a rose, a book, or a pumpkin, but you definitely can get impressions. And that's all those images in a scrying mirror are, anyway. One of the keys to scrying is being able to keep in mind what you want to know about. It's all but required for your subconscious. And what does your subconscious like to help it focus? That's right! Symbols! Which means? Tattoos are great for scrying!

Scrying, on the surface, is incredibly simple. There is one thing I will counsel you on: An altered state of consciousness is incredibly beneficial for this. Luckily, if you practice this enough, you, like me, may find that scrying automatically puts you in a trance. If it's your first time—or seventh—it might help to meditate for a little bit and dim the lights before you start.

So, here is what you need to do. Sit comfortably. Put whatever you're scrying in front of you. If it's a tattoo, position it in front of you, no more than a few feet away. Look at the object with a softened gaze. Once you start staring, bring your question to mind. Keep it there without being forceful. And wait. After a few seconds, a couple minutes, or longer, you may receive impressions. It's that simple.

What is softening your gaze, you ask? It's looking in a way that leaves your eyes more relaxed, not really staring at anything. To practice, take a small-ish object and put it in front of you. Stretch a little bit, and then look at it. Don't stare intently. Just look at it. After a few seconds, I want you to imagine looking at something that is just behind the object. You're still looking in that exact same spot, but not at the object. The object should look a little different now that you aren't staring directly at it. It may be a little blurry at the edges. You might see double. You likely will feel something. For me, it's kind of like the feeling I get when I zone out. Don't soften your gaze and then intensely monitor for any sign something has shifted. That will defeat the purpose. Just relax into it, and be patient with yourself.

When you get impressions, immediately write them down or draw them, and then analyze them. Do any of them have any special meaning for you? Do they make you think of anything? If you're a little stuck, try looking them up in a dream symbolism dictionary. You can also try the automatic writing exercise. There are differences of opinion on how long you should wait before analyzing. I have heard people say you should wait until you've reached normal consciousness, and nothing should interfere with the altered consciousness required for this exercise. To be fair, if you reach a deep enough trance, you might not even be capable of consciously analyzing the impressions! I personally believe that if I have successfully scried, the channel of communication between me and my Higher Self is open, and since I've received a message, I might as well turn it into a dialogue. It's the most likely state of mind where my Higher Self might send other messages or forms of intuition to point me down the right path or add to the message. But that is my preference, built up from my experiences. This difference of opinion is fine; you do what feels correct for you.

If you are well and truly stumped, wait a couple days, and try scrying again. See if you get the same, or different, impressions.

Okay, so here's the little shortcoming of this practice when it comes to tattoos. I said the subconscious thinks in symbols. That's true. If you are scrying a symbol, it makes it easier to keep your question in mind and "focus" on the thing you are scrying about. Of course, when it comes to tattoos, that means what you scry has to be related to the question. Any tattoo that is a symbol of psychism or magick in general would be all-purpose for scrying. Considering scrying mirrors and bowls are traditionally black, a decently sized blackout tattoo would also be all-purpose. Most other tattoos are more limited. If you have just a tattoo of a heart, for example, you might be able to scry about love or health but not much else. Tattoos are always one of the best things because, as I keep saying, of the connection you have with them. But if you don't have a tattoo corresponding to your question, you can always use a different object. There's also nothing keeping you from getting a new tattoo to round things out!

Reducing a Complicated Tattoo for Drawing and Carving

The easiest way to work with a tattoo you have is activating it on your skin. There's no controversy in that. At the same time, I talked plenty about using the tattoo the same way as a sigil, which is frequently drawn, inscribed, or carved. This chapter's spell to become your Ideal Self, for example, explicitly instructs you to carve the tattoo into candles. Using your tattoo as a personal sign also usually requires you to draw your tattoo.

It's up to you whether you want to use your tattoo in ways that require you to draw it. Personally, I do. I like being versatile in how I work magick with my tattoos, and I like working with sigils. However, not all tattoos are as simple to draw as a triple moon tattoo. That design of a flaming skull with snakes coming out the mouth inside a crystal ball? By the time you finish carving it into a candle, you could have made up a bindrune, carved it, and burned the candle to the end. Not very efficient, is it? Also perhaps not as aesthetically pleasing.

So, where does that leave us? As any artist will tell you, any drawing of a person can be reduced to a stick figure. In fact, many people will draw the stick figure before fleshing it out into the person. Just like that, most tattoo designs can be reduced to a "stick figure" you can draw in a few seconds. Provided you can create a "stick figure" that you immediately associate with your tattoo, you can use that as the symbol. It might be more abstract. It might not look as nice. But if you can immediately associate it with your tattoo, magickally speaking, it has done its job.

Every tattoo has a core component—its heart. Some may be easier to see than others. The core component is often the part with the most detail. It's also the place that communicates most strongly the meaning of the tattoo. In a tattoo of a person riding a panther, if you know the tattoo is about harnessing your talents, the cowboy would be the core; if it's about ferocity in battle, it would be the panther. As you probably guessed, any decorative part, such as the flourishes around a coat of arms, would not be the heart. While text is often a key component of a tattoo, if there is an image accompanying it, that might be better to use. Frequently, it is the image that is the symbol; the text is just explaining the symbol. To be fair, though, you could always just write the words in the spell rather than use the image.

If you are stuck and need help finding the heart of your tattoo, do an automatic writing exercise. This time, use the prompt "The core component to my [name of tattoo] is…" You could also use "The most symbolic component of my [name of tattoo] is…," "The center of action of my [name of tattoo] is…," or some such.

Once you have found the core component, ask yourself: "Can this be drawn, as is, in fifteen seconds or less?" If no, zoom in or simplify. Zooming in involves finding a key piece of the core component, a piece that distills the meaning as strongly and as purely, if not more so, while still unmistakenly representing the tattoo. It can also be a piece of the core component that most clearly references what the core is supposed to be. The spots on a cheetah would be a perfect example. Simplifying means making it easier to draw by removing details. The first thing you can think about when simplifying is whether there is anything that is truly unnecessary to include. The seventeen coconuts in the palm tree? Probably not necessary. The random sandcastle added for detail? Probably not necessary. Go through a round or two of that and see how simple you can make it. Then see if you can draw the zoomed-in or simplified version in fifteen seconds. If not, repeat until you've got it.

Now, it may be that your tattoo has a lot of pieces that mean different things. If that's the case, you should break up the tattoo according to meaning. Go back to that tattoo I mentioned of the cowboy riding the panther. The cowboy could be symbolizing your ability to harness and control any difficult situation, and the panther would be your ability to attack any evil that comes near you. In that case, for spells about finding solutions to problems, use a stick figure of the cowboy, and for spells about protection, use a stick figure of the panther.

What if you have a tattoo that is just text? I mentioned a little bit ago that you can write out the message in the candle, on the piece of paper, in the sand, whatever. If it's a very long piece of text and you don't have that much space on your candle, try to make it shorter. A "stick figure" of the text would be finding the one to three words in the message that capture its essence. "Let your faith be bigger than your fear" would be "faith bigger than fear," "faith be bigger," or maybe even just "faith." "The smallest things are the most important" would be "smallest most important" or "smallest are important."

Granted, there are a large number of phrases for which it's hard to make a stick figure. "Strength through struggle" is one. So is "be fearless in the pursuit of what sets your soul on fire." If this is you, there is nothing keeping you from making your tattoo into a chant. Say it repeatedly to raise energy. You can also turn it into a sigil, though it will be more difficult to make the connection between this new symbol and your tattoo.

...

These spells are all meant to be used outside of the tattooing session, but that doesn't mean you can or should work them an hour after your tattoo is done. Especially for any work involving touch, I would wait about four to twelve weeks. That's how long it takes, approximately, to heal fully. In regard to using your tattoo as a personal sign, I would wait at least until your brain is used to seeing the tattoo on you, when your attention doesn't go right to it when it enters your field of vision. That's when your mind has connected it to you, and therefore your sense of self. The amount of time this takes varies.

...

Magick is not the only spiritual activity many of us practice. Some of you work extensively with deities or other spiritual beings. Others do a lot of work with ancestors. If you are one of those people, just as you might not get eight different tattoos for love magick, you might not get tattoos exclusively for spellwork. The next two chapters will give guidance, starting with tattoos for devotional work.

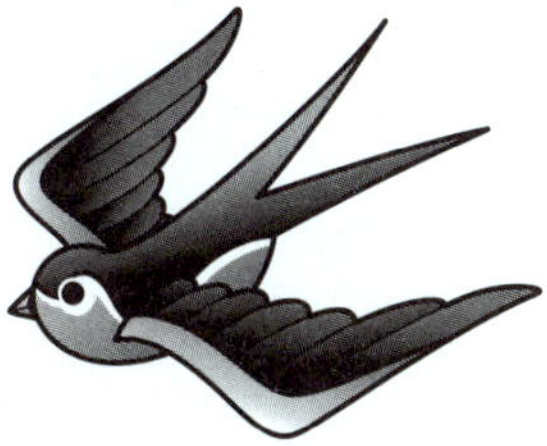

3
Devotional Tattoos

People get tattoos of others all the time, whether it's someone they admire, someone they love, or someone they want to memorialize. Is it inconceivable that you could get a tattoo for a spiritual being rather than a physical being? Whether an elemental, saint, or goddess, you have free reign to create tattoos of magickal beings you like. On a practical level, as you will see, such tattoos are useful for devotional work. They are also helpful when it comes to deepening your relationship with the spiritual or divine being that was tattooed. They are literally a part of you now, after all. You can use the tattoo to make petitions to the being you tattooed and invoke them in ritual more effectively.

The Tattoo as an Offering

Tattoos are expensive, painful, and time-consuming. There are also things people should do regularly to maintain a tattoo, such as applying sunscreen when outside. All of this expense and attention makes tattoos themselves one of the most profound things you can offer to the spiritual being you're tattooing on yourself.

If this is the only reason you want to get the tattoo, I strongly advise you to pay a lot of attention to the design. Yes, in general you should think about how something permanent will look on you. But put extra care into this because it isn't just for you. A half-assed offering is sometimes worse than no offering at all, so take your time. Do your research on the being or deity, making sure all parts are a reflection of them and that every aspect of the design honors them. Choose a tattoo artist whom you already trust or know does quality work. Invite the being to be with you during the session, to experience the love you feel for them in every bit of pain, in every drop of ink. Once you have the tattoo, give it the greatest care you can. Protect it. Make sure it ages well. Make sure every moment you see it you feel pride for having it.

Making Offerings to the Tattoo

Your skin doesn't just sit there and look pretty. There are all sorts of things you put on it, such as soap, sunscreen, moisturizer, and massage oil. Just as you might put some charged water or oils on your devotional altar as an offering, so too can you apply charged water or oils to the tattoo. The tattoo is a link to that spiritual being, after all. That charged liquid is just as valid an offering no matter where it's placed. The special benefit of this practice is that since the tattoo is on you, you always have access to it. Out on the town? You got it. Traveling? You got it. On a camping trip where every cubic inch of space is taken up by food and the tent? You got it. Any moment you want to give an offering, you have it at hand. You can't say the same thing about your devotional altar.

So, what offerings can you give? Obviously, nothing that would hurt you or damage the tattoo. You also want it to be something that can stay on the tattoo for at least a little time. Food offerings are pretty common in general, but what will you do with that piece of sandwich you made for dinner? Mash it against your shoulder and watch it fall off? Thankfully, there are a lot of other things you can use.

Charged Water

For starters, you can charge some water. Ideally, take a bowl of fresh water and stir clockwise. See the energies swirl with the implement you're using to stir and say, "I create this charged water for you, [name of being]. May the energies I pour into it cleanse and consecrate it and form a personal connection to you." Stop stirring. Charge it using energy from your breath. Dip your finger into the water and apply it to the tattoo, circling your finger on the tattoo clockwise. Keep dipping and stirring and swirling until you feel enough has been given.

Of course, you don't always have access to fresh water, or a bowl. In a pinch, grab that half-drunk bottle on the hike and pour a little into the palm of your hand. Use the same incantation, letting your breath charge the water as you speak.

Oil

You can make offerings of oils applied to the tattoo. This has the advantage that you can add essential oils to create many possible bouquets. Oils also have a decent shelf life. And they just feel more special. Charged water is great for the energy you put into it, but it's water on the skin. Oils feel more luxurious. Plus, the scent is transformative. Keep in mind, though, that oils can stain clothes, while water usually doesn't. And you should *not* apply oils before the tattoo has fully healed.

Essential oils don't just smell nice. They are distilled key components of herbs and resins, and many beings, especially deities, have herbs or resins associated with them. They are expensive, though. If you don't want to spend money on true essential oils, you can make an infused oil for a given herb. Pick up the herb from a supermarket, a New Age store, or your garden. If it isn't already dry, put it in a brown paper bag and leave it in your car for a week or so. If it's cold outside, put it in the oven at 180 degrees Fahrenheit until brittle. This bit is important, because wet herbs can make mold. Take however much dried herb you want and put it in at least one and a half times that much oil (e.g., two cups herbs and three cups oil). Let the herbs infuse in the oil for at least a few days before applying. You may want to strain out the herbs, especially if you decided to use a lot in the mixture. It isn't, strictly speaking, necessary though.

I highly recommend that before you start making your oil blend, you put thought into the ingredients. Some deities and even folkloric entities have herbs associated with them but not all, and sometimes you don't have access to them. If this is the case for you, think to yourself: "What are the qualities I associate with this being? What are they known for? What intentions would I call upon them for?" Get out a book and look up herbs that match those qualities and intentions.

When making your blend, you're going to want to start with your primary oil. If you are diluting essential oils into it, it is known as a carrier oil. Not all essential oils are safe undiluted, after all, so you need something to carry them in. Hence the name. Each carrier oil has different correspondences and different shelf lives. Carrier oils don't necessarily have to be used only in blends that align with their intentions. That's just when they shine most. Personally, I use jojoba oil every single time. It's technically a liquid wax, not an oil, so it doesn't really go bad—not for a very long time, at least.

Below you'll find a table of carrier oils, their correspondences, and their shelf lives. Below that is a table of essential oil correspondences. Throughout this book you will see tables of correspondences. These are almost always mine, founded on almost twenty-five years of magickal practice. There is no definitive set of correspondences. No two books will have the exact same list. Whatever associations or connections you make with colors, crystals, herbs, and so on, should take precedence over mine. Use these merely as a guide.

In the case of the carrier oil table, some of the information, particularly information on shelf life, is taken from *The Art of Aromatherapy in Magick* by Dree Amandi Pike and *Blackthorn's Botanical Magic* by Amy Blackthorn.

Carrier Oil Correspondences

Oil	*Intentions*	*Shelf Life*
Apricot kernel oil	Love	One year
Castor oil	Protection, healing	One year
Coconut oil	Love, prosperity, protection	Two years
Grapeseed oil	Beauty, self-care	Four months
Hempseed oil	Psychism, spirituality, prosperity	Six months
Jojoba oil	Resilience, overcoming obstacles	Three or more years
Olive oil	Spirituality, prosperity	One year
Sunflower oil	Success, prosperity	One year
Sweet almond oil	Love, health, wisdom	One year

Essential Oil Correspondences

Oil	*Correspondences*
Basil	Money, fidelity, strength
Cedar	Healing, protection, money
Chamomile	Peace, sleep
Cypress	Mysteries, magick

Essential Oil Correspondences (*continued*)

Oil	*Correspondences*
Frankincense	Spirituality, meditation
Honeysuckle	Money, abundance, comfort
Jasmine	Intuition, magick, love
Lavender	Peace, happiness, love
Rose	Love, healing
Rosemary	Protection, banishing, healing
Vanilla	Love, happiness

While I suggest you try to come up with something unique for the being or deity who is tattooed on you, some of you will have more than one. Hell, some of you will have a virtual pantheon on your body. There could be too many beings there for you to be able to afford making all of them their own oils. If that is the case, I would recommend you use ingredients associated with spirituality in general. These ingredients would include jasmine, sandalwood, and frankincense. If you are going to use true essential oils, please add no more than twelve drops per ounce and no more than three drops if it's a citrus essential oil. Avoid cinnamon essential oil entirely. Both of those can cause chemical burns on the skin, as I said in the previous chapter.

Scrubs

Exfoliating scrubs are an especially nice thing to use as an offering because they take care of the tattoo. It is a myth that exfoliating your tattoo will make it fade. In fact, it will look brighter and crisper because there isn't a layer of dead skin covering it up. In case you forgot from chapter 2, here's how to make a salt scrub. Pour one cup coarse sea salt in a jar, then pour in a quarter cup jojoba or coconut oil and stir until the salt is evenly coated. Add desired herbs or essential oils. If you decide to use essential oils—and you don't have to—use no more than twenty drops. Again, no cinnamon or citrus oils. And absolutely no peppermint oil if the scrub is going even close to sensitive areas of the body.

Making Prayers or Petitions with Your Tattoo

One of the most common things people do with beings they worship is pray. We are used to thinking of prayers as asking for stuff, and if that's all you do, then yes, magick can take care of that well. However, there are all types of prayers, not just petitions. There are prayers that are just meant to worship, such as the Homeric Hymns or the first recorded prayer: the Exultation of Inanna. There are prayers said in gratitude. There are prayers in which one endeavors to be a better worshipper, such as the Wessobrunn Prayer. And then you have prayers that are talking about your day or asking for advice. All of these are valid forms of prayer. All are not magick. And all deepen your relationship to the being or deity you are praying to. Prayer is a subject for an entire book by itself. In fact, many have been written. If you want one, I recommend *A Year of Pagan Prayer* by Barbara Nolan.

You can pray whenever you want. Just start talking, aloud or in your head. But you can feel a greater connection if you are talking *to* something. Try it sometime. Say a prayer to one of your deities one day; the next day, do it while staring directly at one of the statues you have of them or an illustration of them. Does one feel more profound than the other? I will go back again to something I keep saying throughout this book: There are few, if any, connections to the immaterial you can build that are stronger than making it a literal part of you. If you have a tattoo of your deceased grandmother, look at it and talk to it like you would talk to her. Does it feel like you can almost hear her response? She is a part of you now. She is connected through you. Similarly, having a devotional tattoo has the potential to greatly increase the potency of your prayers and conversations with the deity or being.

Sometimes you want to make a prayer and have it stay around. This may especially be when you want to show gratitude or express how much that deity or being means to you. You can create a space for that in your tattoo. Have your tattoo artist draw a fancy bordered area underneath the deity or being's image. Write your message in there. Every time you look, you will be able to see the message of gratitude, of love. That feeling will sink in every time. You'll smile all over again and feel even closer to that deity or being. You can also use the area for making a petition. Write it in the space, and keep it there, knowing it is sinking into the surrounding skin, into the tattoo. It is riding the physical link to them. Wipe it off when it is no longer needed.

Aspecting

If you've conducted a magickal ritual before, you've almost certainly called on some spiritual beings. Calling on the elements, the directions, the guardians of the watchtowers, the Mighty Dead, or deities is pretty common in Pagan magickal rituals. You're more likely used to calling them into the space outside of you. There is also, though, the option of inviting those beings to be inside of you, to take over you. This is an invocation. Some of you may know what I'm about to say: There are few connections that are stronger than one that is literally within you. If you want to invoke a deity or other being, you will have a much easier go of it if they are tattooed on you.

There are two types of invocations. The one you probably thought of first is possession, where the being takes over your body completely. Now, I will say for several faiths, including some African traditions, possession by deities or ancestors is standard sacred work.

Outside of that, it is rare. Instead, people frequently will adopt an intermediate state, where the being is inside them and is encouraged to take some control, but the individual firmly sets that they still have some control over what is happening. This is known as aspecting. You may have heard of aspecting under a different name, such as "assuming a godform." You may also know some common rituals that incorporate aspecting, such as the ritual of drawing down the moon.

Unlike a possession, you have some level of control when you aspect. Also unlike a possession, you might not fully become the deity or other spiritual being. Instead, you might end up with a mix of your personality and the being's. There are several reasons for that, intentional or unintentional. Probably the most likely is you are afraid to give yourself over completely. You don't like the prospect of losing control. That's absolutely understandable; I don't like that either. But you can do some wonderful things when you give up control. If you have problems with giving up control in general, I suggest talking about it with your therapist if you have one. It is a journey I do not feel too qualified to comment on. But perhaps don't bring up possession with them; keep it general.

There are plenty of benefits of aspecting; one of them is that you can take on the characteristics and strengths of that deity or being. I know of one person who would routinely aspect The Morrigan when she needed to be more assertive, especially when she knew she'd be getting into a confrontation. I know of someone else who would aspect Aphrodite when she was arguing with a man she knew who also was a raging womanizer. She used Aphrodite's allure to charm him without overtly flirting so she'd win the argument more often than not. Underhanded? Maybe. But it was his misogynistic tendencies that led him to be so easily charmed that way, so no one is losing sleep over it.

A very important determination of how much of your deity or being comes through during an aspecting is your level of trance. Your mind often becomes quieter in an altered state of consciousness. If you are in a deep enough trance, there is so little noise from your thoughts that a deity can take over completely. If you are in a light trance, though, there are enough of your normal neurons and thoughts firing that it obscures all but the more prominent parts of your deity. Entering a deep trance is necessary for complete aspectings, but it is incredibly difficult and takes a lot of training. Please know, though, that it is possible, and when you one day reach that point, it will be so fulfilling. Also don't fall into the trap of thinking that a complete aspecting is the only one that "counts."

If you are skilled enough at trance work, you can consciously control how much of yourself you give up during an aspecting. If you can't control your trance that well, you can try announcing to the deity or being just how much of yourself you want to retain for the working. Be careful that you're not working with a being with any trickster elements, though.

I would absolutely, highly recommend you talk to the deity or being beforehand if you intend to aspect them. Make sure they are fine with being aspected at this time. You can pray, ask for a sign on a walk, or use your tarot deck. If you get a no, do not go ahead with it. No matter what happens, don't be disappointed if you try and don't feel anything. Greater training might be necessary, they might not want to enter you or don't think you are ready, or you might subconsciously be blocking it. If you dedicate yourself, it is likely you will get there.

How to Aspect with a Devotional Tattoo

There is a traditional method of aspecting using a representation of the deity or being. That representation is always outside of the body, which doesn't work too well for us. I've slightly modified the technique for a tattoo. Keep in mind that you are at least partially turning into another being. You will at least somewhat be adopting their thoughts, mannerisms, speech, and the way they carry themselves.

Step 1: Cleanse and Consecrate Yourself

You are about to let a deity take hold of you. They are used to being in cleansed and sacred space. If you have the time, make sure your body is at least clean and sacred-esque. Take a shower before your ritual and consecrate yourself with blessed water or incense or energy work.

Step 2: Get into Trance

If you are not at a point yet where you can easily get into trance, try meditating or chanting for fifteen minutes. I recommend a meditation that involves focusing on something specific. Keep it in your mind and hold it there. If you find your mind wandering, acknowledge it nonjudgmentally, and go back to the point of focus. Don't call yourself a failure. Don't get mad. Just think something like "Oh, I'm making a lot of thoughts. Anyway, back to it."

Step 3: Gaze at Your Devotional Tattoo

Look at your devotional tattoo. If it would be awkward to do so, especially for how long this might take, I would take a mirror and position it so you can see the tattoo there. See the tattoo as a symbol and emanation of your deity's energy. If you're going to hold the mirror, make sure beforehand that it is light enough to keep in position for several minutes.

Step 4: Announce Your Intention to Aspect

Unlike invocations, what you say here is pretty cut and dry. Just express that you intend to aspect the deity or being and ask humbly for them to merge with you. You might specify at this point whether you want an aspect in which you have more control or one where the deity has more control. Here is an example:

> *Tonight I seek to experience my deity Apollo on a deeper level. Apollo, I ask you to merge with me. Let your divine essence take over me so that I may be a vessel for your beautiful poetry and give you the ability, through me, to impart divine lessons onto others. Take primary control of me, though leave me some semblance of autonomy.*

Step 5: Feel the Being's Essence Emerging and Merging with You

Pay attention to the tattoo area. You should start to feel a tingling or buzzing or warmth. As the sensation emerges, visualize the tattoo beginning to glow. It glows brighter and brighter. At a certain point, the energies in your tattoo will reach their peak. When they do, the sensation begins to spread throughout your body. Feel the energies move within you, shaping you and changing you wherever they spread, melding with you to become a part of you. The way you hold yourself, your posture, the way you subconsciously tense your muscles—that all changes. You know that everywhere the light moves, the essence of this spiritual being is taking over. It spreads over your arms, your legs, your chest. The final place it moves over is your neck and head and into your brain.

Step 6: Breathe

And you have now aspected!

Aspecting is not possession; you do not lose control of yourself. When you wish to end it, send a thought to the being you are aspecting that you are about to be parted from them. Thank them for being with you and for any other task they did while in your body. Then, start chanting, out loud or in your head, "Now is when I'm me again." Feel the presence of the being fade. Stop chanting when you feel fully back to yourself.

Tips on Designing a Devotional Tattoo

Designing a devotional tattoo is a very personal process. Tattooing is permanent, and the deity or being you are tattooing is sacred to you. Therefore, you want to make sure this is done right. Do not rush this process.

Copyrights and Taking Other People's Works

We have all had that moment when we see something and immediately think: "That's it. That's exactly what I've been looking for." Anything else, you won't be as happy with. If you're looking for inspiration for your tattoo and that happens, though, be very cautious. All of these images belong to someone, and many of them are copyrighted. If someone sees you've infringed on their copyright—if, for example, you or your tattoo artist post a picture to social media with it visible—they are able to sue either or both of you. Rare, yes, but it does happen.

Even if there is no copyright, taking without permission is bad. We were all taught this as kids. If you put a lot of time and effort into some art, especially if you're trying to make a living off it, and you see someone pirated the design to make a tattoo, how would you feel? "Flattered" is not necessarily the answer, especially if the tattoo is trash or you like having the agency over your own work to determine how it should be used.

So, what do you do about it? The safest thing to do is talk to the person whose design it is. Lead up front with an offer to compensate them for the ability to use their design. This can take several forms. You might pay them directly, buy some of their art, or give a donation to a charity in their name. There could be something else they ask for; always do what the artist asks of you (within reason). If the design belongs to someone famous, you might have a harder time getting ahold of them, so do a quick search to see if they've ever made any comments about tattoos. If they have a website, look for a "contact" link. If you can't get ahold of someone, don't assume that's a go-ahead.

I would be sure to keep this an open dialogue with your tattoo artist. Be upfront with them. The threat of lawsuits, however rare, makes many of them understandably nervous. In the end, you can always ask them for their take on the design. And if you can't get permission for the design, you can always find something just as good, maybe even better! Ask your artist to help you with this.

Now, specifically when it comes to devotional tattoos, keep in mind that this tattoo is an act of devotion. It is a meaningful sign of the respect you have for that deity or other spiritual being. You need to think to yourself whether it's enough effort to just slap something on that someone else did. If it is, great. If not, that doesn't mean you have to abandon it. It does mean you should examine why you want to use that preexisting work. Do you want it because you have some personal connection to it? For example, were you so moved by *The Birth of Venus* that you were inspired to start working with that goddess? Or maybe it was the cover of your Hellenic Book of Shadows? Or do you want it because it would look cool? Always make sure there is a reverent touch if it's a devotional tattoo because it's sacred. It can be cool without being flippant.

Being or Correspondence?

One of the choices you will have to make as you are planning out this tattoo is how literal you want to be. Do you want to have a tattoo that is an actual depiction of that deity or being? Or an object associated with them? Or maybe even a correspondence? Here are a few things for you to think about:

- *How literal of a person you are:* In high school English classes, did you proudly state that you hate symbolism (the drapes are blue because the author wanted them to be blue, damn it!!)? Or do you like to see how things connect or what deeper meaning they have? If the former, perhaps do a depiction of your deity or spiritual being. If the latter, you might vibe more with a correspondence or an object associated with them.
- *How meaningful any of their correspondences or associated objects are:* Was Cerberus your favorite part of myths involving Hades and the Greek underworld? Did you have a three-headed dog necklace you carried with you everywhere? Did you identify with being the watch dog, protecting your friends? If so, maybe your Hades tattoo should be a Cerberus tattoo.
- *Whether one of that being's associations holds some other meanings for you:* You might not care that Apollo played the lyre. When you work with or worship him, it's as the god of the sun and poetry. But you are a musician, and music is one of the things you hold most dear in this life. Getting a tattoo of Apollo's lyre rather than Apollo himself is getting something with other deep meaning for you. This might create more depth in your connection with Apollo and open new aspects of your relationship. Just be careful that any other associations that hold meaning for you don't take attention away from the deity or other being. This tattoo should be first and foremost devotional.

In addition, it might be helpful to do the automatic writing exercise I've mentioned a few times before. "[Deity or being name] is...." Do you talk about them more in terms of their appearance or personality, or in terms of what they are associated with? When writing about Odin, did you spend the time talking about the tale of him hanging from Yggdrasil? Or did you talk about his one eye and wide-brimmed hat? If you mostly talked about the latter, maybe you're best suited to getting a drawing of him, especially in his guise as the wandering sage. If you mostly talked about Yggdrasil, perhaps you should get a tattoo of the World Tree instead or of Odin hanging from it.

Please note: You should do this exercise for thirty seconds, not three minutes like usual. If you do this for too long, you'll cover all aspects of this deity, which isn't helpful. With a finite amount of time, you'll write what your subconscious thinks is most important.

Getting Inspiration

If you aren't exactly sure what to have in your design, I highly recommend going to the internet. Spend some time searching images. Save the images that speak to you, and make sure you write down somewhere what about it is moving or inspirational. Maybe the face has an expression that matches your being's personality. Maybe the hair is the exact right shade. Maybe the pose is giving the vibe you want the tattoo to capture. Make notes of all the things each image got right and show them to your tattoo artist. Tattoo artists are just that: artists. If you give them inspiration, they should be able to draw something for you. Just give them time and don't be afraid to tell them if something looks off when they show you what they made. I promise they've heard it before. It's better you be sure what is going onto you is exactly what you wanted.

Unverified Personal Gnosis

Many cultures have almost nothing in the way of records about their ancient pagan practices and folk beliefs. Others may have passed down their knowledge orally, so the stories we know today might be absolutely nothing like the stories of a hundred years ago, let alone when they were first told. When someone works with a deity or a folk creature enough, through personal interactions and signs, they might begin to learn new things that fill in those gaps or even contradict previously established belief. This is called unverified personal gnosis (UPG), *gnosis* roughly meaning "knowledge." Let's say you begin to notice that after you work magick with Yemaya you see octopi everywhere, every time. In murals, on TV, in song lyrics … Eventually, when you are praying to her, you hear a request for an octopus figurine to be placed on her altar. You have just developed UPG that Yemaya is associated with octopi.

UPG can be controversial. People don't like taking others at their word in these matters. It also might make people insecure, because who are you to declare what an entire culture did or what a deity likes based on personal thoughts and feelings? I, and many others, believe these experiences are absolutely valid. Everyone has their own way of relating to others and interpreting the world around them. You wouldn't really expect everyone to have the same exact experiences with a deity or other being. Even if this UPG isn't valid for all the people who belong to a faith, it is valid to you and your relationship with this deity or being. Now, if what you learn challenges conventional wisdom about this being, yes, you should probably scrutinize the belief and make sure it's not you making connections that aren't there. But there very well could be many other people who have received this same exact UPG. Even if they haven't, and it's just you, that's fine.

I say this to say if you have some UPG: You may want to put it in your tattoo. That really gives it the personal touch and honors the connection you have. But some of you may be worried that people will judge the tattoo because it is nothing like how the deity or being is typically depicted. Is that deity or being doing something inherently offensive in your tattoo? No? Then people are not likely to have a strong reaction. Besides, I've found fewer people than you think notice tattoos. What is important is that this is your body and this is something important to your relationship with that deity or being.

The only thing to consider is you are going to need some sort of reference for your tattoo artist, and none of the drawings online are going to have UPG built in. Try your best to describe what you want, and be patient with the artist if the first time around they don't capture what you meant. And don't feel self-conscious! Trust me, they've tattooed weirder things than a brownie with warty feet or Thor with a hockey stick.

Keep in Contact with Your Being During the Design Process

You are going to want to make sure that what you put together is something your deity or being would want. It is made primarily for them, after all. You would want to keep in contact and get their sign-off. "Is this something you would be pleased to see me have?" For this, I recommend you use the pendulum. It's a simple device: a weight attached to the end of a string. You hold it up, between your thumb and index finger, and ask questions. The way the pendulum swings determines the answer. You can buy them for about fifteen dollars at your local New Age store or make one yourself by looping some string through a ring or paper clip. Frequently people use it to talk to their subconscious and see how they really feel about a situation. You can also use it for spirit communication, which means you can use it to talk to the being you're getting tattooed.

If you are interested in doing this but don't have any pendulum experience, here is a quick rundown:

When you use the pendulum, the best posture is sitting with the elbow of the arm holding the pendulum on your leg or a table. Your arm should be bent at 45 degrees from the table, and you should be holding the pendulum between your thumb and index finger. You should ask yes or no questions if you're starting out. It's best to keep your questions short and sweet. Better to avoid "not," "can't," and other nullifying words. Before you use the pendulum for anything, your first question should be: "What movement means yes?" Wait to see how it moves. If it doesn't move, that's fine; just keep trying. Once you get movement, you should ask: "What movement means no?" It's then best to complete with what motions mean "maybe" and "I don't know." With that, you know how to interpret the answers to your questions.

I highly recommend you talk to your deity or being often. Make sure you are on the right track. Better to know when things start going wrong than find out from them this isn't the right design and you have no idea what you did wrong. When you talk to them, it always helps to make it a little special. Leave a small offering. Ritualize it, if you want. Give your deity or other being the attention they deserve.

✶ • • • ✶

The final thing I will leave you all with is the fact that for many of you this is an intensely personal tattoo. Magickal folk tend to have deeper, more one-on-one relationships with their deities and other spiritual beings they work with than people in more mainstream faiths. With that in mind, if it feels right to you to do something about, for, or with your tattoo—and it is not illegal—go for it. It's your relationship. The only spiritual relationships that might, on average, be more personal are the ones we have with our departed ancestors. That type of spirit is so special it deserves its own chapter, which we will get to presently.

4
Ancestor Work with Tattoos

Ancestor work, for those of you who aren't familiar with it, is the practice of interacting with, honoring, petitioning, and working magick with your ancestors. It is a powerful and personal spiritual and magickal practice that is widely adopted. I bring up ancestor work in this book because one of the most common types of tattoo is the memorial tattoo. That is a tattoo we get to remember and honor someone who died. Even if you don't have one, you have definitely seen them before. They are the tattoos with two dates. Frequently, they have a halo or wings or hands or a face. Often there is a personal quote, such as "You briefly showed me what love is again" or "We'll see each other soon." These tattoos are among the most meaningful that people can get. They deserve special mention. I can only hope that I give them the honor they deserve in this chapter.

When I say people work with their ancestors, that doesn't just mean parents or grandparents. Ancestors can be your less direct relatives, such as your aunt, your nephew, or your third cousin once-removed. They can be chosen ancestors: unrelated people you knew who have meant something special to you. Like your former neighbor, who was lonely and taught you to love wine when you brought him over for home meals. Your friend's father who showed you how to shave and cheered at your junior league baseball games. Or your first cat who would lie on your lap when you cried. Ancestors can also be people who had a profound impact on your life, whether or not you personally knew them. These could include the founder of the religious sect you belong to, a prominent person of your home culture, or a role model for a hobby you have. Whoever it is, related or not, you can always get a tattoo to remember them—and use that tattoo to work with them spiritually.

What You Can Do with Your Tattoo

As this tattoo is a representation of a loved one, it becomes a taglock, a magickal link between you and them. Just as you might place a photo of your loved one on your nightstand to look at and talk to when you feel you miss them, so can you talk to the "photo" that's been etched into your arm. When you are out and away from home and find you miss them, lift up your sleeve. If your tattoo is somewhere you can't make visible at the moment, rub on the area instead. Start talking. Pour out your feelings, telling them why you miss them, what reminds you of them, what positive things you are remembering. After that, if you want, you can continue going about your day, or you can wait and see if they respond.[55] What you just did was prayer.

In my mind, this type of conversation is even more significant with a tattoo than if you were looking at a photo of them. Why? A photo of them might have been taken when you were never around. You have no obvious link to it. Even if it's a photo of the two of you,

55. If they do, it will likely be thoughts or impressions in your head, rather than a disembodied voice.

that connection is distant through both time and space. On the other hand, your tattoo is on you. This connection you have to them was made when the image was inked on your body, in the here and now. It is personal to you and relevant.

Frequently in prayer, even with our ancestors, we may ask for something. Often people will leave pen and paper at their ancestor altars for physical petitions. But you don't have to go that far or wait until you are back home when there's something you really want. Your tattoo is always with you; let it be your altar. Just as with the devotional tattoo from last chapter, you can devote a space on your skin for important petitions and messages to your ancestor.

You can leave offerings to your ancestor through your tattoo just as you might on your ancestor altar. A small vial of oil can be carried anywhere and by almost anyone (men, you really need to ditch the pockets and start carrying bags). You can go with an oil blend that has traditional correspondences to worship and spirituality. But you have the opportunity, and experiences, to make something more personal. Did your grandfather like to smother everything in olive oil? Add a drop or two to the blend, or use it as your carrier oil. Did you love working on rose bushes with your neighbor? Add a couple drops of rose essential oil. Is there a moisturizer your mother used because she swore it made her youthful? Get a mini vial of that. The best offerings are things that were either very important to them or personalized to your relationship with them. However, if you have a lot of these tattoos, you might not have the space or money for all of those oils. In that case, have something more generic and say some extra nice things as you apply it.

Designing an Ancestor Tattoo

Designing an ancestor tattoo, like a devotional tattoo, is deeply personal. In some cases, primarily with someone you knew while alive, it can be even more personal. On a given day, you might talk to a deity for a few minutes. And every once in a while, you'll do so for an hour or two. You pray, conduct rituals, and get feelings of connection to them or experience synchronicities while out and about. You know their myths. On the other end, if you are fortunate enough to have a good family system, you would be with your parents hours per day growing up. You would see your grandparents, cousins, aunts, and uncles quite often, sometimes weekly.

Even if you only see, or saw, an ancestor a few times a year, you have so many varied, involved, sustained memories and stories that are particular to you and them. These aren't myths that happened to other people. All of these concrete, intimate experiences mean you probably know them more deeply than you do a deity. You know more clearly what your ancestor would or would not like, what they would or would not say. All of this means you might have strong opinions about how your tattoo is supposed to look or how you should try to design it. With that in mind, please know that the design ideas and guidelines I am about to share are not meant to be taken forcefully. This is your tattoo, your practice, your experience. Design it how you want. These are just things to consider.

The only thing I think you must do in this process is make absolute sure your ancestor would be fine with this. A lot of people seem to loosen up a bit after death, but don't assume your extremely conservative Aunt Agnes would appreciate you working pseudo-Witchcraft with her. "What are you doing? Ask God, not me!" Actively try talking to them in prayer or use some divination system to make sure it's okay.

How You Want Them to Be Represented

If you want, you can have a literal depiction of your ancestor. I would argue the most literal depiction is of their face. If you have a lot of tattoos already and don't have much space, or don't want to take up much space at all, you could try their initials. Just make sure that when you look at the tattoo you think first and foremost of them. James Frances Koontz is an example of a name that's not as suited for initialization, with or without the middle name. Rather than a literal depiction, you could tattoo something you associate with them. A bottle of Chanel No. 5 for your bougie aunt. Your father's patron saint. A seagull for your grandmother who always said she wanted to come back as one. Cookies for your childhood friend's older sister who would always make some with you when you had a really bad day.

In the previous chapter, I went over some things to keep in mind when deciding whether you go with a depiction or an association. For ancestor tattoos in particular, there is so much importance in the face. When it comes to a deity or fairy, we technically don't know exactly what they look like, so features can be off a little bit and no one would be the wiser. But say you want someone to tattoo an ancestor's face, maybe Aunt Gertrude, and your artist tattoos your Aunt Gertrude's nose too big? You're going to notice. There's a chance it will bug you. If you read this and think, "Oh, it will be fine. I know my tattoo artist," you might want to be a little cautious. Faces are exceedingly difficult to do well. So difficult, in fact, that what some artists might call a great job, others might think looks bad. So, check out your artist's portfolio, look for tattoos of faces, and decide whether they are up to your standard. With all that being said, again, there is so much importance to the face. The face is more likely to immediately remind you of your ancestor than a tattoo of a bottle of whiskey could. That immediate connection can be very emotionally powerful.

Using Their Ashes in the Ink

You read that right: using their ashes. It may sound a bit morbid, but what better way to honor your ancestor than literally making them a part of you? And what better connection, honestly? This has been a growing practice, and truth be told, in a magickal sense it's kind of neat. You can make whatever tattoo you want, however you like, and with the ashes, it still will be something you can use to honor that ancestor. If you have an ancestor who was a Witch and they gave their blessing before they died or through prayer, their ashes could be an added oomph to any magickal tattoos. If your grandfather liked tattoos a lot, you don't have to get something of his face or the vintage car he liked to drive. Just start putting his ashes in your new tattoos. If he liked tattoos, he would be honored to be a part of yours. Alternatively, get one of the designs he had.

Putting ashes in tattoo ink isn't without controversy. Tattooing is sticking things under the skin. If what you put there is in any way not sterile, you run the risk of infection. And infected tattoos can be bad news, especially if the infection gets in the blood. Ashes, frequently, are not sterile. So, if you ask a tattoo artist to mix ashes you just brought with you in the tattoo ink, they very likely will refuse. Who wants to run the risk of doing that kind of damage to someone? Even if they do mix it in the ink, ash particles are much larger than ink particles, so the ash will just fall to the bottom. All you'll get in your skin is ink. Well, and the bacteria from the ashes.

Now, there is a potential solution. There are companies that specialize in cremated ink. They will re-sterilize the ashes, break them down so the particles won't sink to the bottom, and infuse them in a bottle of ink. I'm not going to lie: The inks are expensive. One bottle will typically run about $250. Then again, tattoos in general are expensive, so maybe this will not be an eye-popping amount to you. Still, it's not something to be done lightly.

If you are thinking of getting a tattoo with someone's ashes in it, *you must make sure your tattoo artist knows*. No one likes surprises, and there isn't really a way to hide this. What are you going to do? Switch the bottles and hope they don't notice it is suddenly a completely different brand? Even if you sent the ashes to a reputable company to sterilize and infuse in the ink, don't hold it against the artist if they still refuse. People have anxieties, and that should be honored. You don't know what they have gone through in the past. They might only be willing to play it safe. If it means that much to you, find a different tattoo artist.

Tattoos for Multiple People

In a later chapter of this book, you will learn about magickally versatile tattoos—tattoos that can be used for multiple, even all, intentions. To borrow a page from that, I'm going to give you ideas for tattoos for multiple ancestors, maybe even all of them. One thing that is essential for this type of ancestor tattoo is an area next to it for you to write the name of the person you are calling. Specificity is essential here, for you *and* the person you are trying to interact with. So however you want—label outline, speech bubble, banner shape—put that ID space in.

Family Tree

Many—but certainly not all—people who practice ancestor work are also into genealogy. These people want to know as much of their family tree as absolutely possible. You might be one of them. If you are, you probably know what the diagram below is. For the rest of you, it's a diagram of your direct ancestors—your parents, their parents, their parents, and their parents, and so on. Rectangles are used to represent male ancestors, ovals are used to represent female ancestors, and diamonds or triangles for non-binary ancestors. This is known as an ancestor chart.

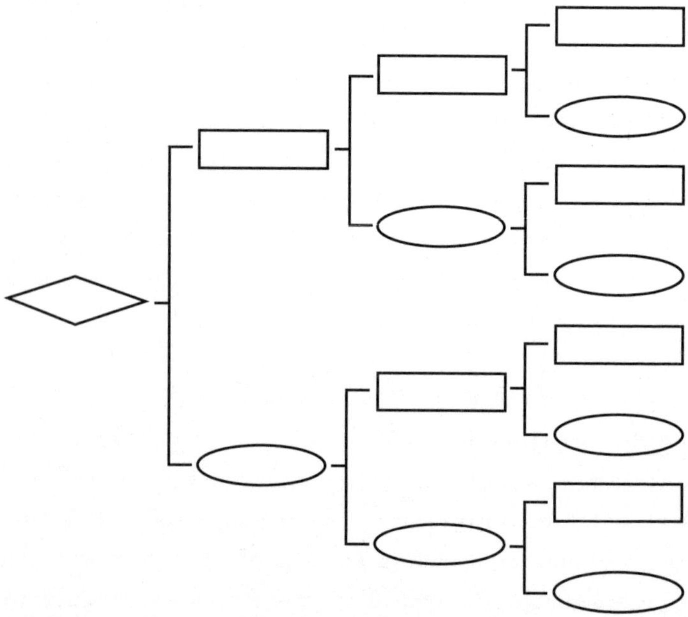

Direct Ancestor Tree

Following is a related diagram that can show extended family. By using a dotted line, you can even include chosen ancestors. A full set of instructions for these diagrams is out of the scope of this book. In a nutshell, though, children get a line going down from their parent or parents to show ancestry. If more than one parent was present, you connect the lines between the parents before going down to the child or children. If only one parent was present, or you don't want to include the other for whatever reason, you just need to make one line. You can go back as many generations as you want.

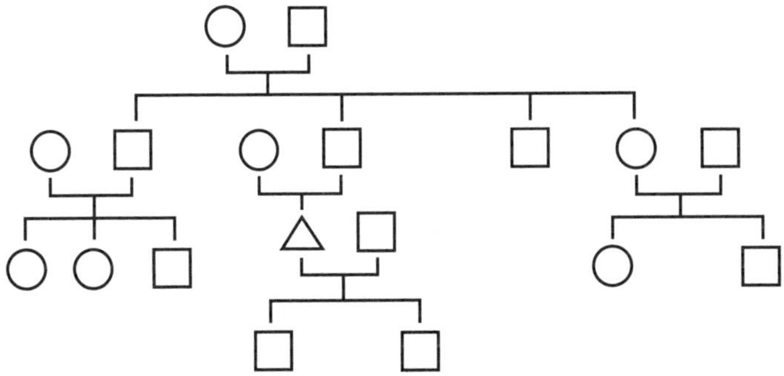

Extended Family Tree

The point here, of course, is that you can use these kinds of tattoos to mark the different people you want to remember and/or work with. There are pros and cons to each diagram. Direct ancestors are only parents and their parents and their parents on down. You may have some beloved ancestors who do not fall into this grouping. On the other hand, you can see the extended family diagram has the potential to get very messy very quickly if you have a fair number of ancestors you would like to call on. The direct tree is very simple and can thus scale to almost any generation you want. To be fair, after four or five generations, even if just focusing on parents of parents, you'll have a lot of shapes you need to match names to. Maybe too many. You could try to tattoo the names next to the shapes, but keep in mind tattoos bleed. You can't have the text and the shapes too small or in several years, all of those will be an unintelligible blur.

Don't forget that tattoos are symbols; you don't have to have one as a literal representation of the ancestors you want to work with. Instead, you can get a tattoo for *all* of your ancestors. Perhaps you can get a tree tattooed on you. It is a fitting metaphor and very magickal for any Green Witches out there. If you do this, though, you really should have the space to name the ancestor you are interacting with.

Mitochondrial Eve and Y-Chromosomal Adam

In your cells are miniature organs that produce energy for the cell called mitochondria. Mitochondria have their own DNA. Unlike the DNA we all know about, which is in the nucleus, mitochondrial DNA doesn't get jumbled up when we have children. Instead, the DNA in our mitochondria is an exact copy of the DNA our mother has. And hers is an exact copy of her mother's. And on and on. As with other DNA, sometimes there is a tiny random mutation when we have children, so the DNA isn't *exactly* the same. But they are rare enough we can catalogue the mutations and figure out around when they happened. This lets us trace the appearance of the mutations through time, taking our mitochondrial DNA back further and further ... to one person.

Yes, it turns out every person who is alive is related to one woman. We first discovered this in the '80s, and the findings have been reproduced through multiple kinds of genetic sleuthing. She has been known by several names, though the media, rather sensationally, has dubbed her "Mitochondrial Eve."[56] A similar situation occurs in men: We inherit an exact copy of our father's Y chromosome—except for the random odd mutation, of course. And by tracking the mutations, we can trace all our Y chromosomal DNA ... to one person. This is a man the media has named "Y-Chromosomal Adam."[57]

These individuals are not actually the Adam and Eve of biblical fame. They probably didn't even live at the same time. Estimates

---

56. Crow, *The Magic in Your Genes*, 97–100.

57. Crow, *The Magic in Your Genes*, 127–30.

suggest Adam lived up to 57,000 years before Eve did.[58] Unlike the biblical Adam and Eve, their existence doesn't mean the population dwindled to a single woman or a single man. Rather, of all the people who lived at the time, they are the only ones whose lineage didn't die out. Think of it this way: You get a small mutation in your Y chromosomal DNA. That mutation is only passed down if you have a son, your son has a son of his own, his son has a son, and so on. How many people have only daughters or no children at all? So, how likely is it your descendants can keep it up for thousands of years? There just happened to be one person who got exceptionally lucky and had the last surviving lineage.

Anyway, school lesson over. The point is we are all descended from one woman and all descended from one man. Not just that, there are parts of our genetics that are more-or-less identical to them. With minor variations, my Y chromosomal DNA is the same as my father's, which is the same as his father's, and so on, right back to one person. It is the same for other men and their fathers. It is the same for all of us, our mitochondrial DNA, and Mitochondrial Eve. We are "identical." We are one. So, in an abstract way, Mitochondrial Eve can represent all women, and Y-Chromosomal Adam can represent all men. You can get a tattoo of her to represent all of your female ancestors and a tattoo of him to represent all of your male ancestors.

···

With this we come to the end of the chapters on what you can do with tattoos that have already healed. But you don't have to wait that long; you can do magick during your tattoo appointment! Really, the

58. Poznik et al., "Sequencing Y Chromosomes Resolves Discrepancy in Time to Common Ancestor of Males Versus Females," 562.

moment you are being tattooed is a great time to cast a spell, as we'll discuss later. We shouldn't rush into it, though. There are things we need to think about before we get to the tattoo appointment itself, whether we're making magick there or not. The first and arguably most important thing is designing the tattoo. Let's keep in mind that when designing a tattoo, you should be thinking about making it correspond to your intention, but you should also make a design that you personally like. While no one is completely consistent, we all have our likes and dislikes with form, and if you really don't like the look of your tattoo, you'll continually regret it. We don't have time for that. We'll explore that now with discovering your tattoo aesthetic.

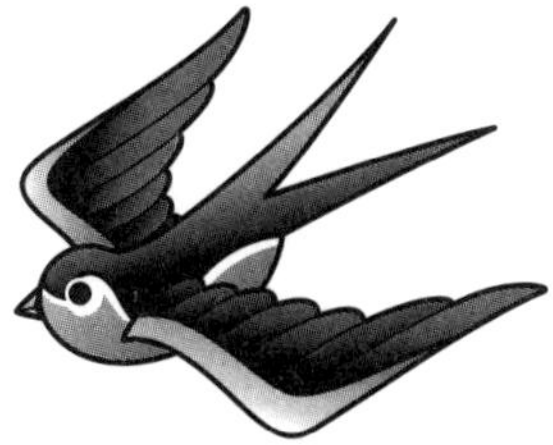

5
Finding Your Tattoo "Aesthetic"

Many Witches have their own preferences when it comes to magick. Personally, I use candles and sigils a lot. Sure, if I did spells only using herbs, I could make it work. But it feels right when there's fire. Most Witches know they have a preference, and they know what it is. Would their magickal tattoos be any different? Personally, my tattoos are all black-and-white, and almost all are geometric; that's the "type" I vibe with best. The tattoos that match this aesthetic are always the ones that feel more powerful. If you have an aesthetic, it behooves you to figure that out before you get other tattoos. You don't have to be a slave to your aesthetic; you don't even need to have an aesthetic. It is a shortcut to getting tattoos that feel more powerful, though. It also helps you figure out what your new tattoo designs might look like. And visually, at least, you'll be less likely to regret the tattoo. I highly recommend you read and think through this chapter before you get to the next one.

So, what might be part of a tattoo aesthetic?

Tattoo Styles

The first thing to keep in mind are the different tattoo styles that exist. By that I don't mean any style that could exist. That would be the same thing as an aesthetic. This is more a list of official classifications, like someone classifying architecture as Gothic, furniture as mid-century modern, or a piece of art as surrealist. Terms such as those are overarching classifications of many of the ways things look and are put together. Not all valid aesthetics, such as "text only," can be found in a list of styles. But it is a start. These are also more or less official. Use any of these terms with your tattoo artist and provided they've been around more than a few weeks, they'll know what you mean.

Of course, any list of styles will inevitably leave some out. But I have some of the more common ones here. Check them out and see whether any of them catch your eye. If none of them resonate with you, that's totally fine; this isn't necessarily the most important part of finding your aesthetic. These styles also aren't all mutually exclusive.

Blackwork: Tattoos that are solely black-and-white. No gray. The amount of black is usually rather large and relies on the spaces without ink to bring out the design.

Dotwork: Tattoos made out of dots, like the name suggests. Usually made just with black.

Geometric: Tattoos made out of or revolving around geometric shapes.

Irezumi: a.k.a. Japanese style. This is the type of tattoo you see on yakuza on TV. It mirrors Japanese woodblock prints from the seventeenth to nineteenth centuries.

Minimalism: A tattoo that has all of the details taken out.

Neotraditional: An evolution of the traditional style. Has more detail and color, though it retains the 2D design. Influenced by art deco and art nouveau movements.

New school: From the '70s. Inspired by the cartoons of the time and graffiti art. On the wacky, distorted side sometimes.

Psychedelic: Looks like an acid trip, deliberately. It's very colorful.

Realism: A good tattoo artist will make realistic depictions. This style takes it to the absolute next level. These are tattoos that look indistinguishable from a photo.

Sketch: Looks like a tattoo done in a sketchbook, though the tattoo itself doesn't have to be simple.

Traditional: The classic Western tattoo style. Bold lines, iconic shapes such as roses and hearts, limited color palette. Remember Ed Hardy T-shirts? That's traditional style.

Tribal: An umbrella term for tattoos done in the vein of any Indigenous style of tattoo. I do not like this term, because there are many Indigenous practices, which can differ wildly between each other. But that is what it's called. It is usually black-and-white.

If there is a particular style you like, and you want to be absolutely sure it is done right, you might look for artists who specialize in that tattoo style. It is true that a good tattoo artist will be able to do multiple styles of tattoos. The best tattoo artists can, too, but they're popular enough they can get away with specializing in one style. They are the people who will do your tattoo best, if the style is important. You can usually tell whether they are the real deal by their photos and social media accounts. If they have more than fifteen thousand followers and most of their tattoos are one style, they are likely to be a specialist.

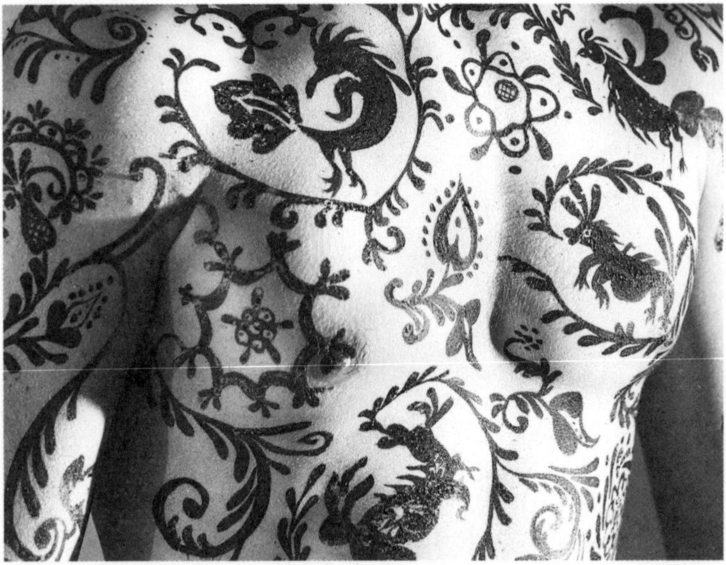

Blackwork

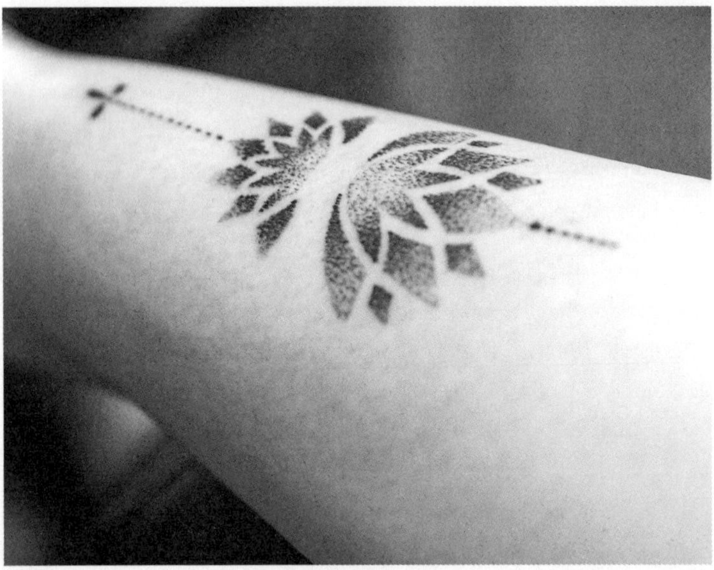

Dotwork

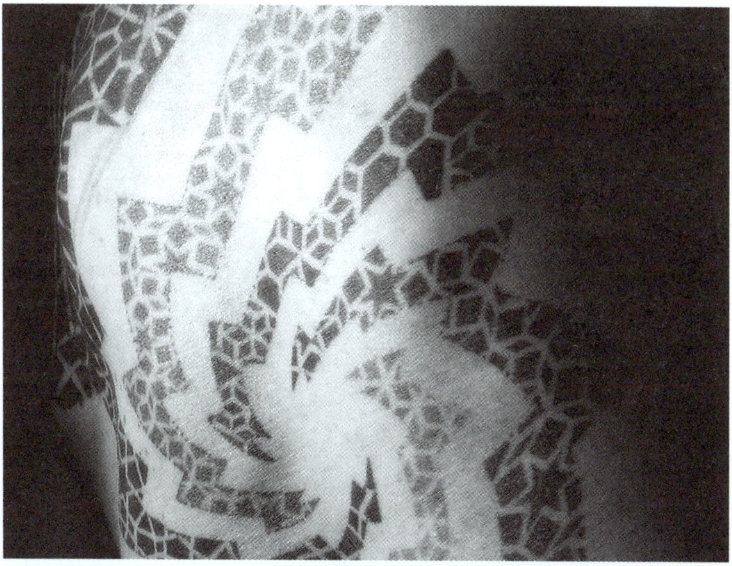

Geometric

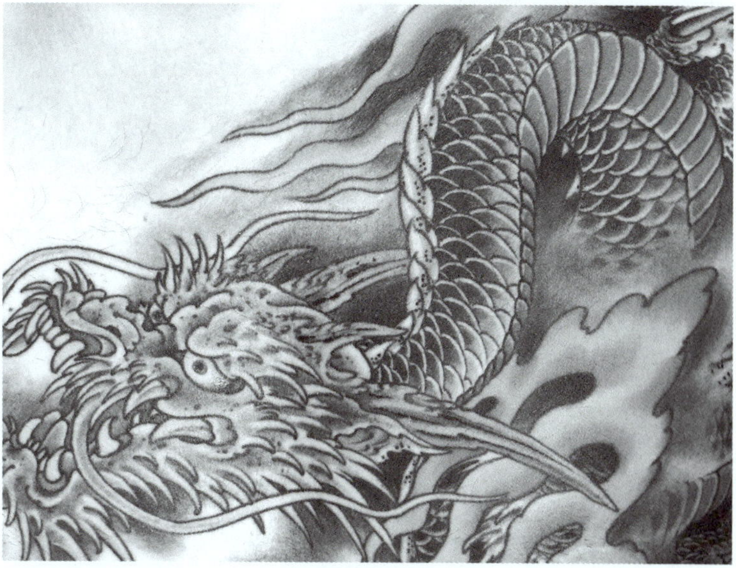

Irezumi

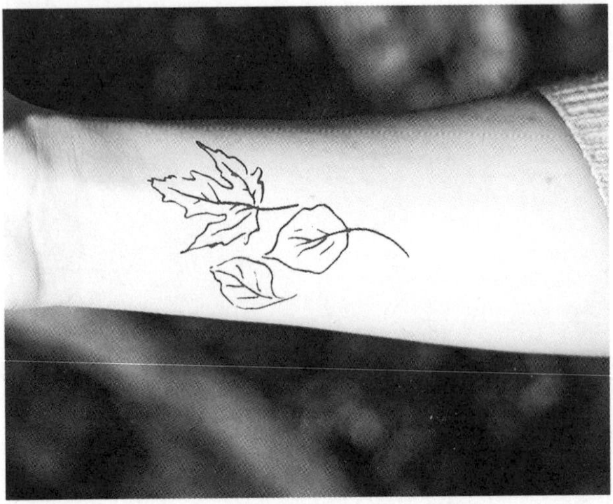

Minimalist

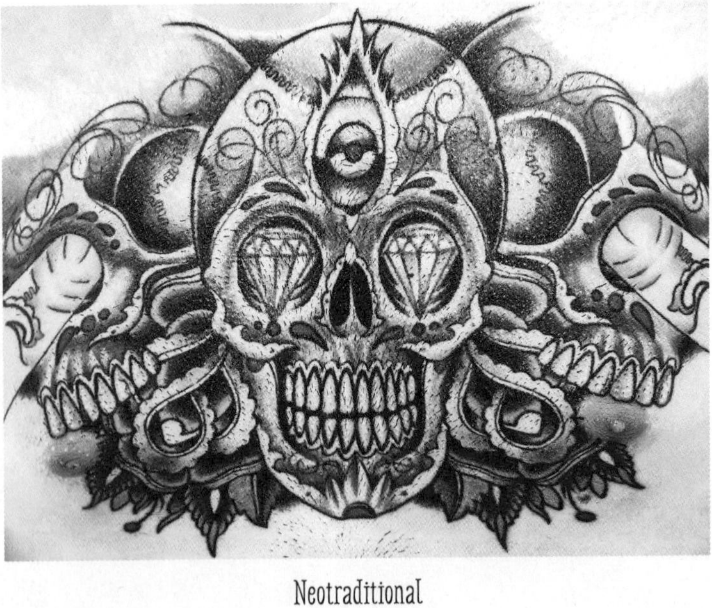

Neotraditional

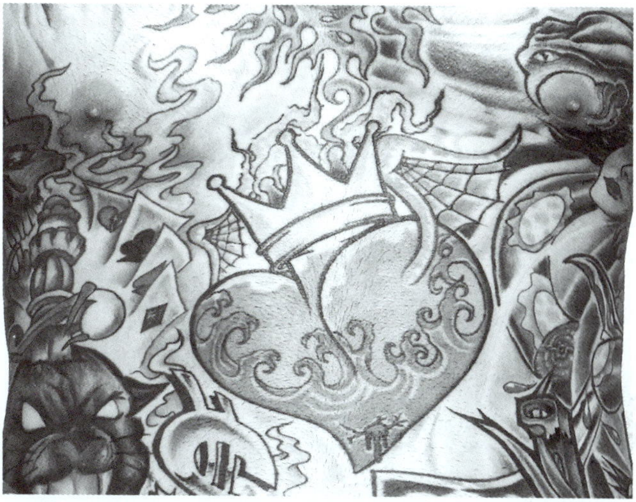

New School

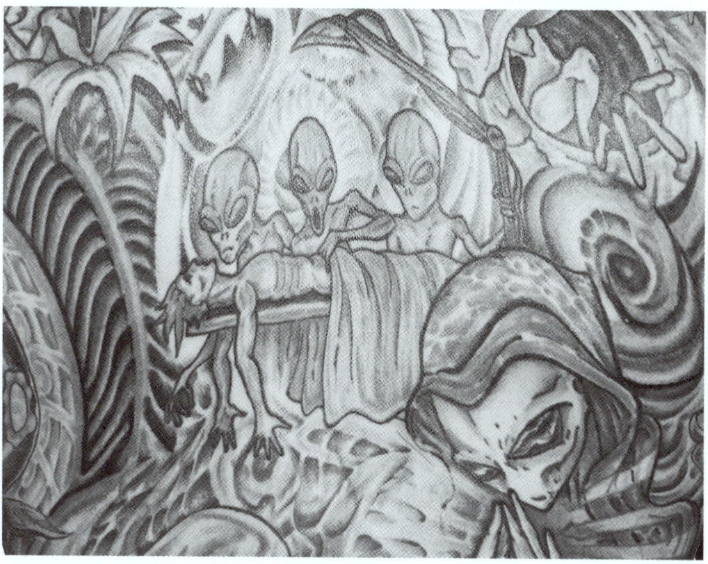

Psychedelic

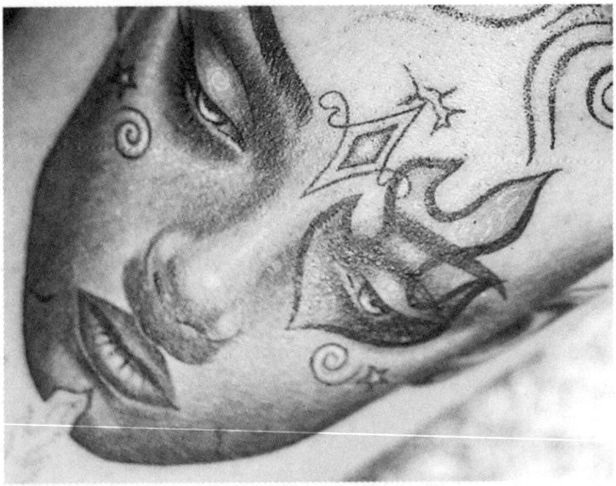

Realism

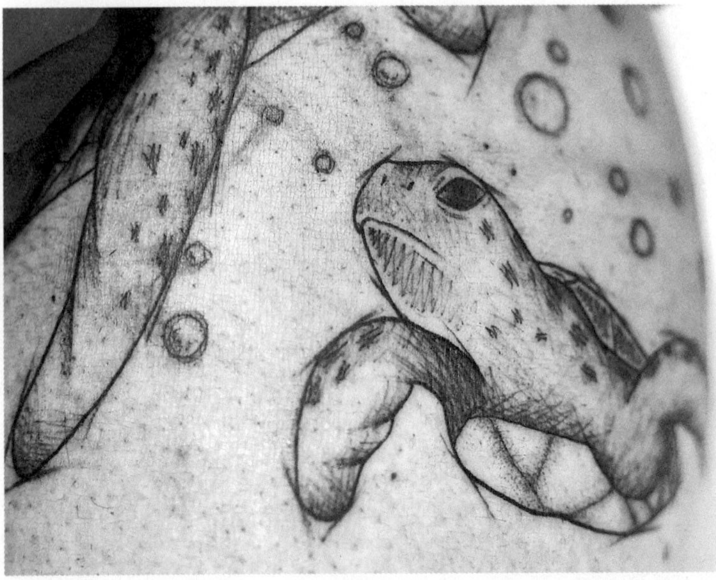

Sketch

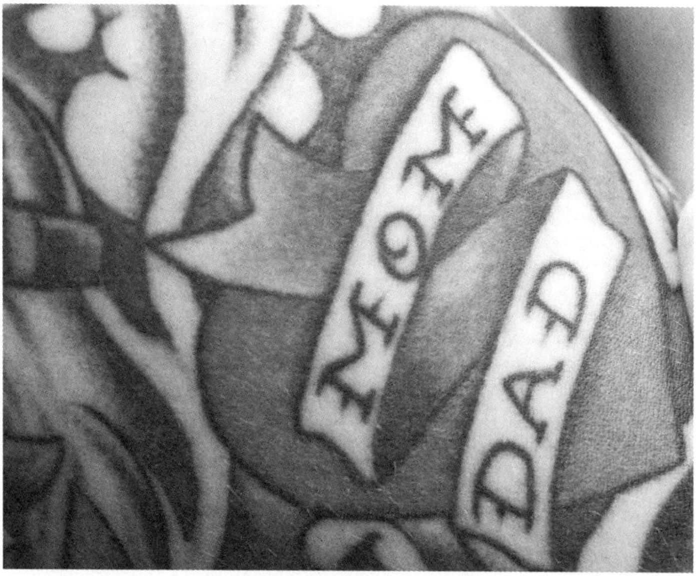

Traditional

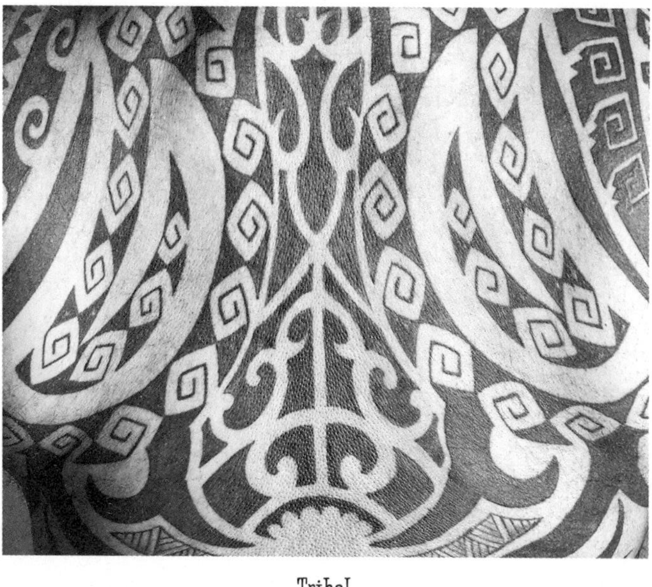

Tribal

Culture of Origin

Do you know your cultural heritage? How dear is it to you? Do you proudly tell everyone you're Italian? Do you try to fly to your ancestral country every year or two? One part of your aesthetic is how much of you should be in it. In other words, what parts of you do you want to shine through? Each culture has a rich set of myths, traditions, and symbols that can find its way into your tattoos. Want a tattoo for addiction recovery? If you're Greek, try the Mati, a symbol that wards against negative influences. Want a tattoo to nurture some self-love? If you're Chinese, try the character for the Chinese element of earth, whose qualities include being nurturing. Want a tattoo for health and longevity? If you're Egyptian, try the ankh! This, of course, isn't anything you're obligated to do. There also might not be a cultural symbol for every intention. But even if it's a common theme among some tattoos, or as many tattoos as you can, it could become part of your aesthetic.

With this, we come to something very thorny, at times even contentious. We don't just love things that come from our heritage; with the rise of globalization, every culture is at our fingertips, waiting to be discovered. Some of us gravitate more than others to a culture other than our own. I have a very good friend, for example, who is obsessed with Japanese culture. They have been to Japan multiple times, they habitually ingest Japanese media, they cook authentic Japanese food, and they import sweets from Japan. They love Japanese culture, and that should be celebrated. But at what point have we moved past celebrating a culture and into cultural appropriation?

Cultural appropriation is a hot-button issue. What is cultural appropriation? When is something cultural appropriation? How bad is it? These are things many people do not always agree on, even within their own culture. A couple days ago, for example, I saw an

Indigenous American scold someone on social media for wearing turquoise, only to have two other Indigenous people defend them. All of this, especially in times such as that, is made even more complicated by the fact that no one, with almost zero exceptions, can speak on behalf of an entire culture. That statement goes both for the people who are offended by someone doing something and for the people who defend them.

So, say you are deeply fascinated by Thai culture. The mythology and practices speak to you on a level nothing else does. Is it bad for you to want to incorporate aspects of Thai culture into your tattoos?

There are no easy answers to this, but I will offer my personal opinion. You are under no obligation to love your culture and your culture alone. That would be ethnocentrism. At the same time, you are not entitled to take the traditions of another if that would mean desecrating them. So, I would tell you to ask yourself at least these questions:

- *Do I respect this culture?* If you don't, leave it alone. How could you like this tattoo if you don't even like the people from whom it came?
- *Is it an act of love and appreciation for the practice?* Doing something because you love the culture and the practice is an act of appreciation and respect. Doing it just because it looks cool or seems fun, knowing there is meaning behind it, is by definition erasing its meaning—especially if you influence other people. And let's face it, everyone influences someone else. This perpetuates the adoption of a meaningful tattoo for aesthetics only. This is how, gradually, meaningful things end up disappearing. It's like yoga, which was originally a pathway for spiritual development. In the Western world, however, the religious aspects have continually

been erased. The result is the most hardcore atheist or fundamentalist can now be comfortable practicing yoga, but any Hindu who wants to build an authentic practice will have a hard time finding more than a teacher who will say "namaste."[59] Getting a tattoo because it looks cool is something that a lot of us do. But if you know the cultural significance, you would do well to get it only if you will honor the full breadth of meaning and significance behind it. If not, there is always another way to design an intention.

- *Will adopting this diminish the ability for people to claim it as an aspect of their culture?* That can take some of the beauty of that culture away from them. This is exactly what happened with tribal tattoos. They are all lumped together. Few people know what design comes from where, and people make up designs and call them "tribal" just because they look like more authentic tattoos. Despite the fact it's called "tribal," I'm not even sure people know that means it's an Indigenous practice. I didn't until I was an adult. And once their heyday ended in the '00s, any person with tribal tattoos was at risk of being called "basic" or "trendy."
- *Am I comfortable answering hard questions?* This might be the most important question of all. Imagine someone comes up to you and says that your arm tattoo was "stolen" from Thai culture, where the tattoo has deep spiritual significance. What do you do? Do you stammer awkwardly and walk away? Or do you say, "Yes, it is a Sak Yant tattoo. Good eye. I love Thai culture. I read about it in middle school, learned Thai in high school, and studied abroad there in college. It is such a big part of my life it feels like

59. Antony, "That's a Stretch," 52–54.

a part of me. I got this in Bangkok so I would never forget my connection to there. I add another one every time I go back. Do you have tattoos like that?" If you're more likely to trip over your words or falter, you're risking encounters that could be very uncomfortable. Even if you think it isn't appropriate for someone to confront you like that, it may happen, and it will be awkward. If these encounters fluster you enough, that might fuel resentment toward your tattoo, so it's probably better to leave that off your aesthetic.

Your Magickal Style

What types of spells do you like to cast? Do you work with sigils a lot? Runes? Herbs? That might influence what tattoo style works for you. Sigils and the geometric tattoo style, for example, go hand in hand. Realism would go well with tattoos of herbs. If you do a lot of astral travel, psychedelic tattoos might be great. When you make spells, are you very by-the-book? Or are you like me and work very much on the fly? If you work on the fly, sketch tattoos might have a nice synchronicity. Are you very no-frills in the components to your spells? Try minimalist tattoos.

Your magickal practices might influence more than which broad "tattoo style" you choose. If you do a lot of astral travel in your magick, you might like to have animal or plant bodies depicted as more fuzzy silhouettes of light. If you work almost exclusively with the elements, you might want the only colors on your body to be red, yellow, green, and blue. If you do a lot of glamours, your tattoos might mainly be faces that correspond to those glamours.

Who You Are as a Person

What do you value? What kind of person do you like to be seen as? Take your time to go over what things you do or do not like. If you have a strong affinity for '90s TV shows, you might build all of your tattoos around characters or props from one of those shows. If you consider yourself a goth, you might just want tattoos that are black, red, or purple. If you absolutely love reading, tattoos of books or book characters would be neat. You want your tattoos to be a reflection of you. All of you.

Has there been a person whose tattoos you saw and immediately felt a connection to? Those types of tattoos, or at least something about the way they were presented, might be a part of your aesthetic. This isn't license to copy something without thought. Instead, take some time to figure out why you felt such a connection to them. When you figure it out, you should be able to distill it into the simple phrase "I like tattoos that ______." If you have that knowledge, you can more easily create tattoos that fit your aesthetic.

Yes, Another Writing Exercise

There are always things I could have missed in this list of considerations. Identity is extremely complex and multifaceted. You might have even missed something yourself. So, let's write! At the top of the paper write: "My tattoo aesthetic is …" You know the rest. Set a three-minute timer and go!

My Example

I consider myself to be a very aesthetic-driven person. I am crazy for clothes. I love to make a splash. My car is purple, for crying out loud. So, when it came time for my fifth tattoo, I decided I needed to keep in mind how all of my tattoos would work together. Here's how I decided on an aesthetic.

From the start, I resolved to do what I could so that if I saw myself with all my tattoos bared, they would all meld together as much as possible. This is pleasing to me and makes it less likely that they will distract from my outfits (priorities!). With that in mind, I started by vowing not to get any tattoos in anything other than black. I also decided to avoid lettering as much as possible because when people see lettering, they automatically start reading it. That tattoo wouldn't meld into the background. There have been times since when I have wanted letters on my body, but whenever that happens, I resolve for it to be in a magickal alphabet, such as Theban, or runic.

For the same reason that I didn't want lettering, I didn't want realism. Literal depictions were out, too. Those are all distracting and would take away from the uniformity of the tattoos on my body. Instead, I wanted to focus on geometric shapes. This is for a few reasons. First, my previous tattoos were shapes. Second, I make a lot of sigils in my magick, but my style is to make them with shapes rather than letters. So, it is a reflection of my magickal style. Third, you can make all sorts of interesting designs for different intentions that are just overlapping shapes.

Finally, I decided not to tattoo my hands, face, or neck. Tattoos are more accepted in the corporate world, but there are still limits. Once office climates have changed, I might get the inside of an ear or my neck done, but until then I am content to get on a virtual call with both my sleeves proudly displayed.

Of course, nothing is set in stone. People frequently change, and there are always exceptions. You don't have to hold fast to your aesthetic. It's just a guide. But the guide will make the next part easier: actually making a design to cover your intention. We'll go over that now.

6
Designing Your Magickal Tattoo

I will freely admit that I am very much a by-the-seat-of-my-pants person when it comes to magick. I will make things up as I go along. Just this past weekend—two days ago, actually—I did a spell for happiness and lasting connections. It was glorious. One of my favorites. But I basically just went into my ritual room and through each drawer of both magickal cabinets and my cases of crystals and tarot decks (I'm a hoarder, but it's fine: hoarding sparks joy for me), thinking, "What do I have for lasting connections ..." I grabbed candles of several different colors, three different herbs, a couple essential oils that seemed fitting, and some crystals. On my way out to get to my partner's place, I spotted a decorative piece on one of my bookshelves that seemed to be an appropriate representation. I grabbed that, too. While setting up the altar, which was my partner's kitchen island, I spotted a piece of amethyst jewelry just lying there that could double as a pendulum. Perfect. I made the chant up on the spot, which I coupled with the pendulum swinging to raise energy.

Oh, did I mention I knew for three weeks I wanted to do this spell?

Sound chaotic? It definitely is. I would consider it a personal achievement if some of you ceremonial magicians fainted while reading that. It definitely isn't everyone's cup of tea, but it works for me. And it comes from decades of experience; I know enough to not have to plan anything out ahead of time or even have appropriate supplies. Just throw me in a stuffed closet, and I'll come out with a miniature harp, a cat whisker, three coins, and an extremely annoyed pixie for a prosperity spell.

One of the few times when I am not this chaotic? Tattoos. Especially magickal tattoos. I can cast almost any spell and in five minutes take apart the altar and put away the supplies. No one would ever know it happened. Can't do that with tattoos. Tattoos are permanent. If any other spell didn't go quite as planned, I could do it over again. I can't really "do it over" with tattoo magick. Yes, one of the last chapters of this book is about cover-ups and reversing tattoo spells. No, I do not want to spend all that money on it. So, tattoo design is one of the few instances I will spend time planning my magick.

I realize a few of you who are new to tattoos might start reading this the night before your appointment. If you have a design already, are confident it's the right design for the magickal intention, and are certain there's nothing about it you'll regret, you're good. Read through this at your leisure. If not, now is not the time for the tattoo. Contact your tattoo artist and ask if you can reschedule. Even if they have a cancellation fee for the night before, it's going to be worth it. Your tattoo artist knows these are permanent and not to be entered into lightly. They'll understand; just don't make a habit of it.

This is not the most important chapter in this book. It is definitely up there, though, so I highly recommend you take your time reading this, especially if you don't have a lot of tattoos. The one exception is if your tattoo artist only does intuitive tattooing, which is using intuition to decide what your tattoo design should look like.

If they exclusively do intuitive tattooing this chapter won't be necessary, other than maybe setting your intention (sometimes intuitive tattooers will decide that for you too). If you don't know whether your tattoo artist is an intuitive tattooer, you should ask. They usually have to be very vocal about it, though, on the off chance someone books them not knowing, gets pissed, and writes a bad review.

Step 1: Set Your Intention

If this tattoo is going to be used in magick, you need to set your intention for the tattoo. Knowing what the tattoo will be used for is going to guide your design. If you realize halfway through you want to tweak your intention, you might have to start the design over again. So, let's do what we can to get it right the first time. Most of you have made intentions before, so I'm not going to belabor it. I just have two things for you to keep in mind.

Make Sure It's Something You Want

Yes, you can reverse a spell, even a tattoo spell (see chapter 12). Reversing a tattoo, though? That's a different animal. Laser removal doesn't work as well as people think it does. You could cover the tattoo up instead, but they still cost as much as the first tattoo, if not more. They tend not to look as good. And you may have to go through multiple laser removal sessions anyway just to get the tattoo light enough for the new ink they're putting in. You're much better off putting in effort to make sure the intention you come up with is something you actually want.

Assuming you already have a pendulum, or are buying one based on how much I've talked about them, this would be a perfect time to use it to speak to your subconscious. When you think you have your intention written down correctly, ask your subconscious if this is the right intention for this tattoo. While you're at it, ask whether it's what you genuinely want. If the pendulum says no, that doesn't mean you have to scrap the idea completely. It might mean that the intention needs to be tweaked to truly align with what you want.

It's better to give an example. Say you think you want a love spell to attract the perfect woman for a relationship. Now, love could be exactly what you want. However, there are a lot of different kinds of love. Maybe you want a wild fling. Or a friend. Or the love a pet can provide. You did say "perfect woman"; perhaps you're actually looking for the perfect man or the perfect person. You also said "relationship." You might want a relationship but only one that leads to marriage. If you asked the pendulum if the intention you came up with ("attract the perfect woman for a relationship") is something you genuinely wanted, it would say no. It's too easy to think, "Well, clearly that means I don't want a love spell" and do something completely different. If you had done something completely different, though, and hadn't done some digging with your pendulum, you would have missed a love intention that could have been very beneficial for you.

In figuring out where or whether to tweak your intention, it is best to start general and get increasingly specific. Love is the overarching theme, so you would start by asking, "Do I really want love?" If no, scrap this intention. If yes, ask if romantic love is the kind of love you're seeking. If no, go through other types of love. If yes, go on to the other parts: gender and outcome. Every time you make a tweak, you can ask the pendulum whether this is now the correct intention. In each case, I would not be satisfied with a yes. Don't think a yes means you only want romantic love. Ask, "Is there another type of love I would genuinely want in my life?" Or, "Is there another type of love I should do a spell for?" If yes, figure out which that is, and then ask your subconscious which you should work on first.

Are You Working Magick with This Outside the Tattooing Session?

Let's say you want to do a spell to protect your wife while she is working her construction job. After thinking about it, you decide you want to do the spell with a tattoo. You got a hard hat over a pickup truck, with her initials on top. You cast the spell during the tattoo appointment, because there's no time like the present. It works like a charm. Three months later, your brother is going overseas to serve in the army. You now need to do some protection magick for him. Would you be able to use your tattoo? Would you be able to look at that hard hat, that initialed tattoo, and use it to work protection for your brother too?

When designing your tattoo, ask yourself when and how you'll be working with it. Will you use it often or seldomly? Are you going to use it in a very narrow set of circumstances, such as physical endurance during marathon runs? Or would you want to be more general, perhaps using it for health or protection? You should keep in mind that spells require focus, and that comes from appropriate symbolism. For your mind to appropriately use the symbolism to focus your spell, you want to make sure that it reflects as many facets of your intention as possible. The more you can bring in all the pieces to a specific or complex intention, the better the mind can focus. Also, as much as possible, avoid symbolism that makes you think of something completely different. That can make you lose focus.

With that, my general guidance is: If the tattoo is definitely a one-time thing, or it is meant for a very specific set of circumstances, go nuts. Be as specific as you possibly could want to be with the design. On the other hand, the more often you plan to work with the tattoo, the more you will want a more generalized design. The more spells you cast, the more variety there will be across those spells.

The more variety, the broader you have to make the tattoo to vibe with them all. From the example, if you will only use your tattoo for protecting your wife, the design I mentioned would work very well because it is personalized to her. If you already know you might also want protection for other people or things and you will use that particular tattoo for it, you will want to design it around a more general "protection" intention.

Some of you probably already have a tattoo that's just as specific, if not more, as the one in my example. Don't panic yet. There still is an association with "protection" in the tattoo I talked about. You just need to play up "protection" in a more general form. That's just changing the association, which you do by pairing new things with it. Use the tattoo in protection magick, and often. The uniting factor between all of the spells is protection in general, so the tattoo will be associated with that. The more you use it, the stronger the association becomes. The first time you might need to have your brother's picture next to the tattoo or write his name above it. That way your brain goes, "Oh, for my brother, not my wife. Got it." The next time, when you need to protect your home, you might draw a house around the tattoo so your mind goes, "Oh yes, for the house." All the while, though, the spell for your wife, the spell for your brother, and the spell for the house are all for protection, so the association with "protection" keeps being reinforced, while the associations with your wife occur less and less. Your brain will start thinking of protection more, and your wife less, making the association stronger for more general spells. Soon you won't even need additional props. Your pendulum will tell you when.

Step 2: Determine Placement

Sometimes the design naturally comes to you before you think about placement. But it's definitely a good idea to determine where the tattoo will be placed before thinking about design. This is important, because placement will determine size and relative shape. A rib tattoo usually is going to be longer than it is wide. You don't want it to be so wide that you can't see all of it if you're looking straight at your side. If you're going to do your arm and you think you're going to be squeamish about the pain, you need to be conscious of the elbow and the crook of the elbow. You'll want to modify the design so you can miss that area entirely since it's one of the more painful areas. A butt tattoo is going to look very different if you're getting it on the rounded part versus on the side. Leg tattoos can be bigger than arm tattoos.

Placement will determine size, and size will help determine how detailed you can make it. The ink in your tattoos will migrate over time. Lines will get blurred. A tiny full moon will eventually become an unfocused gray circle. If you want a highly detailed tattoo, it will have to be on a very large surface. On the flip side, if the only place you think you can put a tattoo is your wrist, you'll know you can't get away with having something extremely intricate.

There are a few non-magickal considerations when you determine the placement of the tattoo. The first consideration is pain. If you are squeamish, avoid your ribs, neck, elbow, knee, and shin. The second consideration is visibility. If you don't want it to be visible in the workplace, you can't do your neck, face, or hands—not the first three to six inches of your arm, even. Button-downs and blouses don't always sit nicely on your wrist. The third consideration is free space. This could mean space free of tattoos. It could also be space free of scars, because scar tissue hurts more than regular skin. It could also be space free enough of hair that you can see it. It likely should mean free of moles because it's harder to detect skin cancer when the skin is dyed a different color.

On a magickal level, different body parts correspond to different intentions and facilitate different spells. It does make sense that body parts have correspondences. Your neck, for example, will govern communication and leadership because that's where your voice box is. Your legs will govern stability because they are what allows you to stand upright. On a more practical level, if you're going to be activating the tattoo with touch, make sure it's on an area you can reach. If it is something you want to use all the time, even while out, make it on your arms, which is the most visible body part when out and about. If you are going to be inscribing it in spells, place it somewhere you don't need a mirror to see it. This is especially important if you're not good at reversing a mirror image in your head.

The following table shows the correspondences for different parts of the body. You can use it alongside any non-magickal considerations when thinking about placement. If you can't place the tattoo on the body part with the perfect correspondence, work with what you have. Magickal correspondences are more about giving your tattoo extra oomph. They won't hinder you. I would prioritize the non-magickal considerations when figuring out placement, anyway. I want to feel good about the tattoo and the magick. A suboptimal placement won't ruin your magick, but it could make the tattoo look like shit.

Body Part Correspondences

Body Part	*Correspondence*
Head	Wisdom, problem-solving
Neck	Communication, leadership, support, stability, open-mindedness
Shoulders	Power, wealth
Chest	Support, love (especially above the heart), empathy (especially above the heart), fertility

Body Part	*Correspondence*
Ribs	Protection, banishing, healing
Stomach	Feeling centered, balance, understanding yourself, accessing your personal power, wealth
Back	Support, strength, banishing
Genital area	Love, fertility, creativity
Legs	Support, stability, perseverance, healing
Feet	Grounding, perseverance
Biceps	Strength, protection, power
Triceps	Support, balance
Forearm	Magick (in general), spirituality, protection
Wrist	Life, healing, fertility
Hand	Magick (in general), power, strength, communication, flexibility, creativity

Step 3: Make Your Design

Now we go to the actual design! If you'd like, you can just tattoo the outcome you want, but that really limits you. It looks a lot cooler if you find a design that can represent the parts of your intention.

This process will look a little different depending on how your intention is set up. If it is relatively simple, the process is as easy as making representations of the parts of your intention and fitting them together. If you have an extremely complicated intention or an intention with lots of detail, you will want to make the essence of your intention the core of the tattoo and then build the rest of the details around the core component. This prevents the design from getting messy and aimless. In either case, you will need to find representations for the concepts that make up your intention. The easiest way to do that is to think about correspondences. This gives you the symbolism for your subconscious to seize on. Below is a table with correspondences for different intentions. You can use it as a jumping-off point. If you aren't finding what you need in this table and are feeling too overwhelmed to come up with your own answer, I recommend checking out *Llewellyn's Complete Book of Correspondences* by Sandra Kynes.

Keep in mind there are always ways to layer on symbolism. If you're going for "get money" as your intention, you could choose *coin* from the table below and call it a day. Or you could add to it by incorporating a color and a number. Have eight of them and make them gold.[60] For love, you could have a heart shape. You could also have a comet or a comet whose tail is five pink hearts one after another.

Tattoo Intention Correspondences

Intention	*Correspondences*
Balance	Gray, indigo (cosmic blue), number 2, Libra, scales, symmetry
Banishing	Black, Saturn, skulls, wind, fires, barbed wire, giant *X* (perhaps over something else)
Calm	Light blue, pastels, number 4, Pisces, waves, peace sign, lavender
Adjusting to change	Brown, number 2 or 5, the moon, Pluto, frogs or other amphibians, chameleon, compass, diamond
Confidence	Purple, orange, the sun, Aries, Leo, chicken, peacock, tiger
Courage	Orange, red, number 1, Mars, Aries, honey badger, lion, rainbow

60. There's no such thing as metallic-colored ink, but your artist has tricks to get close to it.

Intention	*Correspondences*
Creativity	Yellow, pink, rainbow, number 9, Neptune, Leo, Aquarius, paintbrush, artist's palette, the Muses, beaver, parrot, treble clef
Divination/psychism	Light purple, silver, the moon, crystal ball, eye, the Norns, undines, a thread
Controlling emotions	Blue, number 6, the moon, water, crabs, a cup (that is not full or overflowing), undines, dragonfly
Endurance	Indigo, brown, rusty red, Mars, Taurus, camels, horses, evergreen trees, anchor, cactus, diamond
Enlightenment	Purple, pearlescence, Pisces, Buddha, bodhi tree, lotus, dragon, dragonfly, stars, diamond
Fertility	Green, number 3, the sun, Venus, grain, rabbits, pregnant woman, Earth Goddess
Friends, seeking	Blue, numbers 2 and 3, Venus, Gemini, Sagittarius, Leo, dog, otter, glasses clinking
Happiness	Yellow, peach, the sun, sunshine, butterfly, songbird, phoenix, smiley face
Healing	Green, blue, lavender, turquoise, the moon, Cancer, wells, hot springs, waterfalls, dove, dolphin
Health	Green, red, apple, dumbbell, curled bicep, pyramid, stethoscope, plus sign, caduceus, horse
Knowledge	Apple, books, scrolls, quill pen, glasses, diploma, atom, spaceship

Tattoo Intention Correspondences (*continued*)

Intention	*Correspondences*
Learning	Light blue, yellow, number 7, Mercury, Gemini, Sagittarius, books, swords, rolled up paper, glasses, pen, raven, sphinx
Love	Pink, number 5, heart shapes, Venus, Cancer (romantic), Scorpio (sexual), comet, rabbits, peacock, rose, water
Luck	Green, orange, numbers 4 and 9, Jupiter, four-leaf clover, horseshoe, rabbit, unicorn, rainbow, playing card
Magick (general)	Black, purple, silver, number 13, the moon, apple (esp. cut with the star seeds shown), wand, pentacle, stars, owl, raven, wheel
Money/abundance	Green, yellow, number 8, Jupiter, Capricorn, Taurus, grain, dollar signs, coins, bee
Protection	Red, black, thorn, shield, armor, wolf, armadillo, salamander (the magickal being), safe
Renewal	Black, red, the moon, Pluto, Scorpio, phoenix, egg, snake
Spirituality	Purple, white, dark blue, number 11, Jupiter, Neptune, Aquarius, Pisces, candle, religious symbols, rays of light, dove, aura
Stability	Brown, gray, red, number 4, Saturn, the sun, Capricorn, cow/bull, turtle, evergreen trees, mountains

Intention	*Correspondences*
Strength	Red, brown, number 4, Mars, Taurus, bicep, barbell, horse, bear, gorilla, griffin, thunderbird, diamond
Success	Orange, yellow, royal purple, the sun, Jupiter, Capricorn, dollar signs, diploma
Transformation	Black, purple, pink, orange, Pluto, the moon, Scorpio, snake, butterfly, dragonfly, moth, diamond

Obviously this is not an exhaustive list. You might not find anything on here that really speaks to you. In that case, I suggest—wait for it!—an automatic writing exercise. This time use the prompt "The representation of [concept] of my [intention] tattoo will look like…" or "[Concept] to me looks like…" or "The most meaningful way to show [concept] in my tattoo is…"

Designing If the Intention Is Relatively Simple

Take your intention and highlight any word that is a description, a verb, or a noun. Cross out any synonyms. Cross out anything that would be unnecessary to put in the tattoo. Then find a representation for each of the highlighted parts and a way to make them all fit together. Layer on the symbolism if you want, perhaps coloring an object to correspond to a nuance in your intention.

If your intention is one noun and has one or more adjectives for that noun, the noun would likely be the central component, and the adjectives would be revolving around the representation of that noun. Same thing for a noun and a verb, though you can show the action, too. A "perpetual good health" tattoo might include an apple for good health. You wouldn't make it, say, brown for stability or perpetuity because a brown apple is rotten. But "perpetual" brings to mind the symbol for infinity. So maybe there is an apple in the process of getting peeled in one long ribbon, and the peel is wrapping around itself to form an infinity sign. "Creative music writing" might be a musical note, colored rainbow for creativity. "Finding friends" might be an otter in a magnifying glass. If you were to show the action, you can have two or more otters playing.

Finally, we make stylistic choices if there's nothing left to do from an intention-setting standpoint. You might think your spirit communication skull tattoo looks a little bare; if you want it to look cooler, this is where you would add the flames and red eyes. You would add any flourishes like smoke or filigree here too. You would also incorporate the tattoo style.

Designing If the Intention Is Very Complicated or Has Lots of Detail

Every complicated intention has its essence. When thinking about your design, you want to start with representing the essence. Once you have that, you can branch out into other aspects of your intention. For a simple, broad intention, you already know the essence. A love tattoo's essence is love. A strength tattoo's essence is strength. For more complicated intentions, it is frequently what your spell would be categorized as at a high level. For example, if your intention is "I want to have three children who are genetic descendants of me," the high-level version of your intention would be "fertility." If it's "I want to ensure I always interpret the tarot correctly for others," the high-level version would be "psychism." If it's "I want to get over my childhood traumas and face the world as a stronger person," the essence would be "healing." Perhaps also "strength," but you are becoming stronger because you are healing your childhood traumas.

Healing is the mechanism, so "healing" would be the more appropriate essence.

The part of your tattoo that contains the essence of your intention is its "heart." The heart of your tattoo doesn't have to just be an object. You might really want a butterfly tattoo, but you just moved to a new place and you really need to find new friends. Do you have to give up the butterfly for a friend-finding tattoo? Not necessarily. Just make sure the butterfly is blue, and if you want, have two or three of them flying around each other. Then build the rest of the intention around them. As long as you know it's a friendship tattoo when you look at it, you're good. Your aesthetic might also affect what can and cannot be the heart of your tattoo. Mine can't be a color because I only do black. If your aesthetic is animals, you will want the heart of your tattoo to be an animal, not a household item or a weapon.

The final step is to take the heart of the tattoo and build out representations of the rest of the intention around it. It's pretty important to create the heart first because with a bunch of items to find representations for, things can get very difficult to coordinate. This makes it easier and makes sure the essence of the intention shines through. If you plan to use this for magick later, it might be better to keep the tattoo more high-level and incorporate the specifics in your visualization during the session. If that's the case, you might stop after you find a suitable representation for your tattoo's essence.

For "I want to meet the love of my life when I move to San Francisco," you might have chosen a heart shape for the core of your tattoo, or maybe you went with a depiction of water. Let's riff on "water" for the rest of the intention. The San Francisco bit would be an iconic part of the city, such as the Golden Gate Bridge. The bridge can also symbolize bringing two people together. The core of your tattoo fits very nicely here, because the bridge goes over water. So be sure the water under the bridge is visible. To show "of my life," put a sun on the left and a moon on the right and shade the sky to show that it's a transition from day to night. The stages of the day is a not-infrequent metaphor for the stages of one's life. By having both together, it's symbolizing the bridge and water will exist from now until you die.

To see what detail you should add in for your intention, highlight any word that is a description, a verb, or a noun. Cross out any words that are synonyms for the essence of your intention, which you already put into the core of your tattoo. Cross out anything that would be unnecessary to put in the tattoo. Then find a symbolic way to incorporate everything highlighted in your tattoo. If you are having a lot of trouble with one of the details, either try again with a different representation of the intention's essence or ask yourself if you need that detail.

Let's use, as an example, "I want to find a buttload of money during my scuba diving trip to the Caribbean this summer and live in comfort for the rest of my life." Your essence was "money," which you think you could symbolize with eight golden coins. So, let's take out anything that isn't a description, verb, or noun, or the essence of your tattoo. That leaves "find," "buttload," "scuba diving trip," "Caribbean," "this summer," "live in comfort," and "rest of my life." There are times when multiple parts can be summed up in the same image. If you think about it, if you were going on a scuba diving trip, where would people be looking for money? Underwater, most likely! I mean, do people go scuba diving anywhere else? So then why not have the tattoo be you actually finding the money underwater in your scuba suit? Put the money in a chest, because when people think underwater treasure, they think pirate chest. You can make there be eight visible golden coins when the chest lid is up to maintain the symbolism, but the fact that it's an entire chest means there's a lot more underneath. That way, Fate won't trick you by having you find exactly eight coins.

Okay so that takes care of "find," "scuba diving trip," and "buttload" since there would be a buttload of coins in the chest. That leaves "Caribbean," "this summer," "live in comfort," and "rest of my life." People associate islands and palm trees with the Caribbean. So, at the surface of the water, have a little island in the distance with a palm tree. The rest of this is trickier, but the phrase "live in comfort" implies both money and security or stability. Security and stability are associated with squares ... what else is that shape ... paintings are. Oh! The scene could be a painting with the square as the frame! Make it a really nice painting frame to imply money. If this is a painting, then maybe at the corner there is an artist's signature and the year. Make that year this year, because the painting wouldn't be made until after you found the treasure. That way you've covered "this summer." And for "rest of my life," people look at paintings, don't they? So have an older version of yourself staring at the painting. This implies you're still rich enough to afford the fancy frame. If you want to be extra careful about "rest of my life," give the older you some high-end designer clothes.

...

This is only one of many systems for designing a tattoo. If you have a system that works better for you, go right ahead with that. The only thing I will suggest regardless is to check in with your subconscious throughout this entire process. I cannot stress that enough. Don't just use your pendulum for the intention portion. If you are lucky, when you see the final design, there will be a click, and you will know beyond doubt this is what it should look like. For anything less certain, use the pendulum. This is a complicated process, so I have a few examples for you over the next couple pages.

Example 1: "I Want to Connect with My Higher Self"

Aesthetic: Minimalist, black-and-white,
no tattoos on the head

This will be a relatively simple tattoo. You need something that corresponds to "you," something that corresponds to "Higher Self," and something to connect them. This will be placed on the forearm, since we can't put any tattoos on the head, which corresponds to magick and spirituality.

Minimalist tattoos do not, by their nature, have much detail, so we can't go all out with this. In that case, the lowest hanging fruit for "you" might be a literal depiction. Now, what do we know about our Higher Self? It's expansive, both within us and without, a link to the Divine, ethereal, a part of the fabric of the Universe ... so what corresponds to expansive, fabric of the Universe ... a star? A planet maybe? A star or planet might be nice. A star is sometimes hard to translate, though. It's possible, but let's try planet first. An ethereal planet might be a gas giant or have rings. So maybe a planet that looks like Saturn or Neptune. So, you could have you, a ringed planet, and some dots between the two for connection. OR! You could replace your head with the Neptune planet. Human torso and ringed planet head. That needs very little detail, so it is perfect for minimalism. And having it as the head symbolizes that the Higher Self is at least partially within you.

Example 2: "I Want Stability in Uncertain Times"

Aesthetic: Realism, natural objects,
muted colors

So. Your company is going through rounds of layoffs. Your doctor told you a test came back weird, and they ordered seven more. Your partner and you are looking for a new house because of a mold issue, and your parents are now getting a divorce. You need to be able to go within to find stability. In these uncertain times, you need a rock to hold on to until everything else settles down.

The essence, of course, is "stability." You don't want to go big with this tattoo and don't want it on your back because you don't want this to translate symbolically into lying around when you should be up and working to mitigate uncertainty. You choose your leg, not just for support but also perseverance. Looking at the list of correspondences for "stability," we see evergreen trees and mountains. That goes with your aesthetic of natural objects.

If we wanted to, we could end there. Stability is by nature long-lasting, so it will be there during uncertain times whether we specify in our tattoo design or not. This wouldn't be a good example, though, would it? Now, when things are uncertain, we can't see through to the other side, almost like we're staring through a fog... A fog! But we can't have the tree or mountain within the fog. That's almost as if the uncertainty overwhelms your stability. But we can have it rising above the fog. For extra stability, we can have four trees or four mountains. If the tattoo is going on the leg, that might not be enough space for four mountains depicted realistically, as with your tattoo aesthetic. So, we'll go with four evergreen trees rising above the fog.

Example 3: "I Want a Successful Career"

Aesthetic: Psychedelic tattoos, astronomy, astrology

There are *so many* ways to make a successful career tattoo. The key for you is that you don't want a successful career for one year. You want a successful career that lasts your entire working life. An era, if you will. But how to depict an era?

If you are a fan of astrology, you may have heard of the Age of Aquarius. This comes from the astronomical phenomenon the precession of the equinoxes. The earth's axis wobbles in such a way that, over time, the position of the sun and bodies appear to move against the stars. Every year on the spring equinox, the position of the sun against the zodiac moves ever so slightly westward. Over about 26,000 years, it moves throughout the zodiac. Right now, at the spring equinox, the sun has Pisces in the background but is about to be in front of Aquarius. Astrologically we are moving from the Age of Pisces, then, into the Age of Aquarius, where the roughly 2,200-year era will be ruled by that sign's energies. This is where the phrase "New Age" comes from, by the way.

Anyway, if you want to bring about a successful career era, what better way to depict that than putting the Age of Capricorn on your body? If you are a fan of psychedelic tattoos, have a psychedelic depiction of the sun and Capricorn playing with each other. Now, that might be just a depiction of the sun in Capricorn, so we need to make a connection to the spring equinox. Eggs are associated with the spring equinox, and they symbolize new life or beginnings, just like how tattooing the Age of Capricorn is your beginning of a successful career. To give more opportunity for psychedelic touches, and connect to the spring equinox better, have the egg be painted and cracked open so the sun and Capricorn are almost rising out of it. With all of these details, it is probably better to have it on your back. Put it closer to your shoulders for wealth.

Example 4: A Couple's Wedding Tattoo

Aesthetic: You prefer sketch style; your partner prefers blackwork, including and especially blackouts

Rings are so passé and easily lost. If you really want to show commitment, get a tattoo. You and your partner are about to get married and want a tattoo that represents happiness, fertility, stability, love, and a passionate sex life. You both also want it to be visible because you aren't intending to hide your love. Even if you are eschewing wedding rings, there is nothing like the symbolism of a band or circle to represent eternity. Obviously there will be too much detail for a ring finger. A thigh might be good for stability, but you both want this to be visible, so maybe wrapping around your bicep and triceps. It isn't the best corresponding body part, but that isn't a big deal. It doesn't harm the tattoo magick in any way. And honestly the triceps works with its themes of support and balance, two things that are necessary in relationships.

Obviously this isn't just going to be a band, especially not with all of the symbolism we want to incorporate. This is also going to be a complicated intention. What is its essence? Probably "love." "Commitment" might also work, since a wedding is a commitment ceremony. So "lifelong commitment." Remember what I said earlier in the chapter about the sun and moon being all stages of the day and therefore all stages of life? That would work. And you would have the two of you throughout the tattoo to symbolize lifelong commitment. There is the core of your tattoo.

If the core of the tattoo is day into the night, that goes well with outside. This then might lend itself to a series of nature symbolisms. And the band can double as the ground in the scene. So, we start with the rising sun, which is also a symbol of happiness. We'll eventually get to children, which you two want in this scenario, but we need to start with a group of two things that represent friendship and love and sex life. Songbirds! Not just birds but singing birds, because that's a mating call. We can have two songbirds flying around each other and a musical note coming from one to show song. If we want to get deep in the symbolism, we can have them singing over a rose bush.

A little bit to the right, for love and sex life again but much more importantly fertility, we could have two rabbits outside their burrow. For continued stability, we would have a tree after that. Maybe the burrow can lead down below the band, underneath the tree! To the right, trees are excellent places to have picnics, so we could have two people there with a basket and a couple small children. That way you can continue to pull in the theme of fertility and your life goals. If we are going to incorporate the bit about showing all parts of the day, we are going to need a night sky somewhere after that. The couple could be in the daytime but pointing to the constellations to evoke continuity and a sense of wonder.

Now, you and your partner have different aesthetics. Is that an issue? Do you have to compromise? No. The styles won't hide that they're depicting the same thing. The style differing is just adding flavor and a touch of your individuality to it. And the scene does lend itself relatively well to both. Blackwork/blackout just means that this will all be in silhouette. Some of the important smaller details, such as the roses in the rose bush, will likely be untattooed, because the ink will eventually blur out the small details.

···

I recognize that some of you, especially if you don't have much free money or skin to tattoo, are probably hesitant to make a design for a single intention, even one as broad as "love" or "money." Why be "wasteful" when there's only so much you can give? That's totally fine. In fact, I'll give you a solution in the next chapter, when I talk about magickally versatile tattoos. Those are tattoos that can be used for multiple intentions.

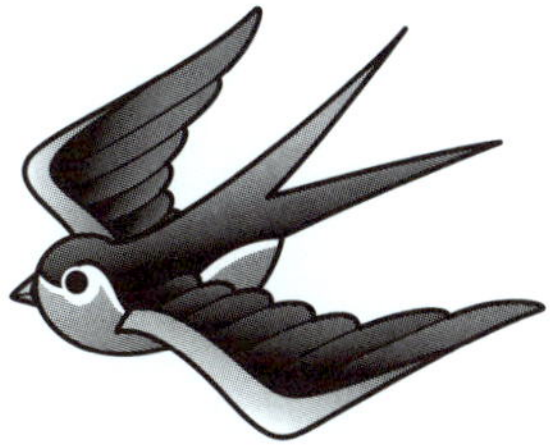

7
Magickally Versatile Tattoos

I know at least a fair number of you are thinking there are a lot of spells you want to cast. You don't want to have to cover your entire body to get them all done. Tattoos take time. They're expensive. You want more bang for your buck. What you can do is get a magickally versatile tattoo—one that covers a lot of intentions. These are honestly my favorite. I don't have as much of an issue with time and skin coverage as other people might, but I prefer these because they are just plain efficient. They have a lot of reusability value after the tattooing session. I also know I don't have to worry about not having a tattoo for my intention. I'm going to be honest, creating a tattoo that covers a wide variety of intentions could mean you have to get a little creative. But I can give you a head start, and a lot of examples, by sharing the five overarching types of tattoos I know of that cover multiple intentions. These are the power sign, the void, the encyclopedia, the matrix, and the devotional.

Despite the fact that this kind of tattoo is my favorite, there are pros and cons to magickally versatile tattoos. This kind of tattoo is definitely versatile, efficient, and reusable. At the same time, it is a little harder to establish a connection with an intention. When it comes to a one-off tattoo, you spent a while coming up with the design, used the same visualization while being tattooed, and use it for—more or less—the same thing in the future. There is a lot of time, attention, and energy directed to one concept, which makes the connection that much stronger. You don't quite get the same thing out of activating the elemental symbol of fire in your elements tattoo for a creativity project one day, passion the next day, and transformation and sexuality the day after that. You don't get the same thing out of a sigil you just made up and inscribed in a matrix tattoo, which had a different sigil last week and a different one the week before.

Then again, you usually do that with your spells, don't you? You frequently don't use the same sigil for every spell; you make one up. You may work with the same element for a lot of different things, you may put together herb combinations you may not have used before, and you may make a completely new crystal grid every time. And unlike many of these spells, you don't need special access to a magickal cabinet of supplies; you take your tattoo with you. Even if you don't think you like the concept of magickally versatile tattoos, I still highly recommend you read this chapter and keep an open mind.

The Power Sign

The power sign is relatively self-explanatory: It's a tattoo that represents magick or power. This could be a symbol characterizing your personal connection to your power or magick. It can also be a symbol that you and many others associate with power and magick. As always, there are trade-offs. It's much easier to come up with a popular power symbol. Many of you might have one of them tattooed on you already! The personal power sign, though, can be preferable because it has more significance for you.

Personal Power Sign

A tattoo that represents your personal power can take several forms. It could be a tattoo that represents you in general; a tattoo that represents you in a magickal context; a symbol that has personal connections to the concepts of power and magick; or a tattoo that represents a formative, powerful magickal experience. I have a friend who has a bindrune of his name tattooed on his wrist. He put the symbol together decades before he got the tattoo, right when he started practicing Witchcraft. Through that entire time, it has been a symbol to him of the foundations of his power. In his case, the tattoo represents him in a magickal context, as it is made up of runes that are a very solid part of his practice. It also is a tattoo that represents a formative, powerful magickal experience. He created the sigil when he first started practicing Witchcraft, to go on the box that housed the runes he made. Finishing that box was the first time he truly felt like a Witch.

Please keep in mind that this kind of tattoo doesn't need to be that profound or moving. It does have the potential to be quite meaningful, but we don't all have those kinds of experiences. It doesn't make you less of a Witch if you can't think of anything like that. It can be as simple as a tattoo of your wand or a magickal necklace you used to wear. It can be a tree you used to read under in the park or a flashlight for those times as a kid you'd read books on Paganism under the covers. Maybe it's a beach for the place you like to go to when you cast spells, the opening line of the circle-casting chant you made up and use in each ritual, the date you were first initiated into your coven, your magickal name if you or someone else gave you one... If all else fails, tattoo your name in a magickal alphabet such as Theban.

General Power Sign

Tattoos don't have to have some great personal meaning. How many of us have gotten a tattoo because we thought it looked cool? I know a lot of you have a triple moon tattoo or the words "as above, so below" on your leg or arm. Tattoo designs that are traditionally associated with power, or are magickal symbols, by definition can be used as a source of power for every intention. Sure, it doesn't have that deep connection that a personally meaningful tattoo might have. It doesn't mean the tattoo is any less powerful, though. It all depends on how you treat it. If you treat it with reverence, if you view it as a representation of power or magick, you can make that link. Provided you treat your tattoo as sacred, it can be quite effective as a magickal tool.

I have a pentacle at the very top of the sleeve of my right arm. It represents the source of my power and therefore amplifies any energies I put forward when I work with the tattoo. At the very start of my journey, in high school, I wore this symbol proudly on my jewelry. It was a signifier of the power of Witchcraft and the ability to succeed in repressive environments. It's always been a power symbol for me. I could have used a different symbol to represent my power. I did think about making a sigil. I thought about making an eclipse because I associate the new moon with magick, rather than the full moon. In the end, though, I realized that my sleeve, which is already very in-your-face with a bunch of sigils, deserved to be crowned with something that is very in-your-face. There is a lot of power behind being bold and open. And there is no symbol that people associate more with magick than the pentacle. Also, I thought it looked cool.

The Void

A lot of mythology includes stories, usually creation myths, in which something is made out of nothing. This nothingness, which has the potential to make anything, is sometimes called the void. That potential makes the void magickally charged, and a void tattoo is a representation of its infinite potential. This, therefore, means it can make anything and is usable for any intention. My blackout sleeve would be good as a void tattoo, if I wanted to use it that way. An outlined circle is also absolutely fine. No one said the void had to be black. Just make sure there is nothing within the border of the void.

The key with this type of tattoo is that you associate it with the void. A circle tattoo could just be a circle. It's the intention behind it that matters. You can heighten the association first by keeping that intention in mind during the tattooing. You could also add symbolism around it to make it clear this is the void. You could ring it with different species of seeds, since seeds also represent formlessness and potential. If you mean for your tattoo to represent the concept of Wyrd, perhaps place runes around it, even spelling out "Wyrd" with runes. I associate magick with the new moon rather than the full moon because it is a void. If you like that idea, you could add crescent moons on all sides of the tattoo, since the crescent moons are the phases immediately on either side of the new moon. If you want to be extra careful to distinguish this from the triple moon symbols, make sure the circle is black for the new moon. Also, you might have the crescents facing the opposite direction that they do for the triple moon symbol. If you are reading left to right, or past to future, you would want a waning crescent to the left of your new moon, not a waxing crescent like with the triple moon. But that is up to you.

To use a void tattoo, you could rub oil over the tattoo or activate it any way you would another tattoo. Like a pentacle or other power symbol, it can work with any intention. Keep in mind, though, that unlike a pentacle, the void is a space out of which things are made. The best way to use it, then, is to draw or write your intention within the tattoo. That act is a microcosm of your intention manifesting. As above, so below. Just take a marker and write or draw your intention mindfully, paying attention to the sensation of every stroke of the marker while you visualize. Once you have done that, activate it in your usual way. If your void tattoo is a blackout, it looks really cool to draw your intention on it in a silver or gold marker.

The Encyclopedia

An encyclopedia tattoo, similar to its namesake, has every intention represented within it. Obviously, it can't contain every conceivable intention. You'd eventually run out of skin. But you can have representations of all the broad intentions: love, money, healing, protection, and so on. The easiest example, of course, would be writing down on your body one word for each intention. You could then activate the proper intention in your spellwork. That doesn't look very cool, though, does it? Don't worry. We can fix that by using visual representations of each intent. If you wanted, you could use popular representations: Make a heart for love, a dollar sign for money, a shield for protection, and so on. More abstract and personal correspondences, such as the Monopoly man for money, also work. Finding a way to put them all in one bigger design is nice so you get a sense of cohesion looking at them.

The most abstract form of an encyclopedia tattoo is one made with representations of each intention that are part of some larger group so they are naturally associated. I realize that definition was also quite abstract. Don't worry. I'll give an example: a horn of plenty, out of which spills several different herbs, such as lavender, sunflower, peppermint, and rosemary. This is an encyclopedia tattoo because the correspondences of those herbs cover all of the major intentions. The tattoo could also not spell out every intention but rather depict a system of magick that can represent every intention. Draw out symbols for the four elements. Within the four are any intentions you can think of; you just have to pick the right element for the intention. If you are very celestially minded, you could have the symbols for each of the planets and choose the planet that governs your intention. You could also tattoo a rainbow wheel containing all the colors. There are so many possibilities.

What I did for the encyclopedia tattoo on my arm was create a sigil for the categories of magick I have worked with. Protection, healing, banishing, and so on. There are twelve in total. They're tattooed on my arm in three-by-three patches with a spiraling line moving through each of them down to my wrist. When I activate a sigil, I also activate the spiral, tracing it down to my wrist and then to my index finger. With that I create a path of energy the sigil can follow out through my hand.

I have another tattoo on my leg that could theoretically also be an encyclopedia tattoo: the letters of the alphabet, in runic, in a half circle. That is only part of the tattoo. The entire tattoo is supposed to be a pendulum board, with the runic alphabet to be used like a spirit board but with a pendulum. But if I wanted, I could use it for magick by dangling my pendulum over the correct rune and visualizing while twirling the pendulum around it. I personally don't connect with it that well; a bindrune is much better for me. Also, in hindsight, I am rarely in shorts and can't easily use the tattoo. But I had no room on my arms, so better than nothing! At the very least, it works well as a pendulum board and looks absolutely awesome!

This type of versatile tattoo matches up really well with your magickal practices if you tend to be less eclectic. Systems of practice, more or less, are meant to be comprehensive. There is a color for any intention, an herb for any intention, a rune for any intention, a planetary spirit for any intention, and so on. So, if there is a type of magick you like to use often, I would encourage you to see how you could incorporate it into an encyclopedia tattoo. If you like sigils specifically, this might also fall under the type of tattoo I'm going to talk about next.

The Matrix

A matrix, basically, is something that other things can be created in, partially because it contains the structure to make them in. Below is the Web of Wyrd. It's known for being a structure that can contain any rune. You can draw any rune you want in there for any intention, such as Wunjo for romantic connections, Lagaz for psychic development, or Fehu for a new job. But wait, there's more! You can probably see that no matter which rune you choose, there is still some space left in the web that might fit others. You can put an entire bindrune in there! There are space limitations in this particular example, but that doesn't matter because you can expand the concept out. Add more columns, more diagonal lines, so you have more freedom to create whatever you want. And you're able to do it because this tattoo provides the structure to make it.

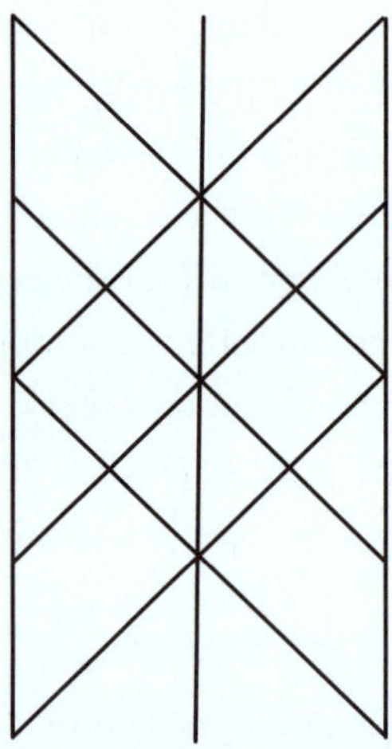

Web of Wyrd

You've possibly seen someone in real life or on social media with a honeycomb tattoo. If you want to get one, maybe try out a pattern like this for size:

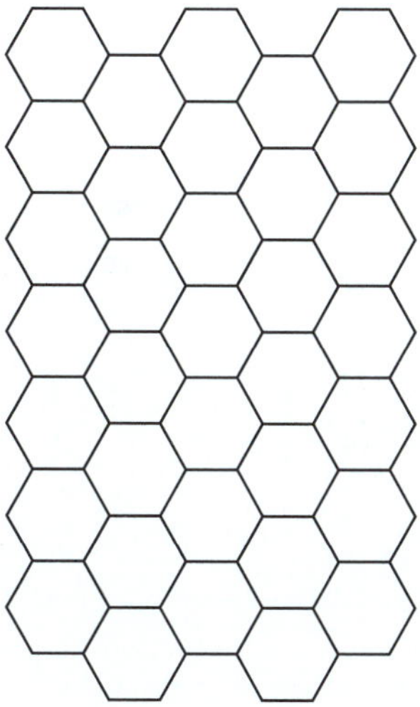

Honeycomb Tattoo

Notice anything? If not, try making lines connecting the honeycombs that share a side. Make sure the line goes through the center of each honeycomb. If you do that, you'll see this honeycomb also has the structure to make bindrunes. You can make bindrunes by coloring in the honeycombs or simply drawing lines through them. It's its own Web of Wyrd! The honeycomb pattern works for more than just bindrunes, even. If you have enough small honeycombs, you can treat them like pixels on a computer screen. Color each one in to create a grainy picture, perhaps of your spell's outcome.

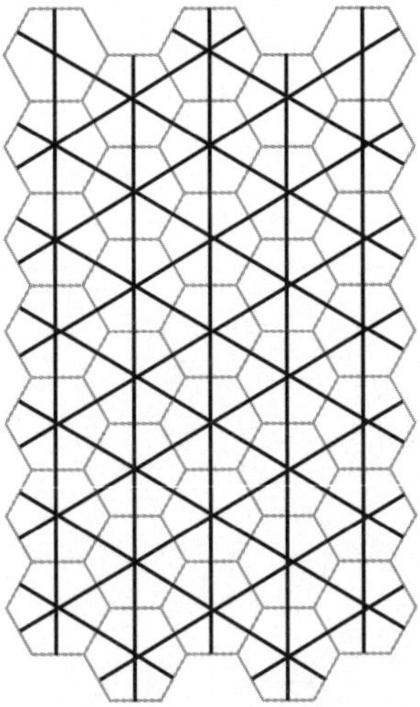

Honeycomb Web of Wyrd

My final example is a sigil matrix tattoo, which I actually have, except mine is in Theban. Look at this picture, which is the letters of the alphabet put into a circle, in order.

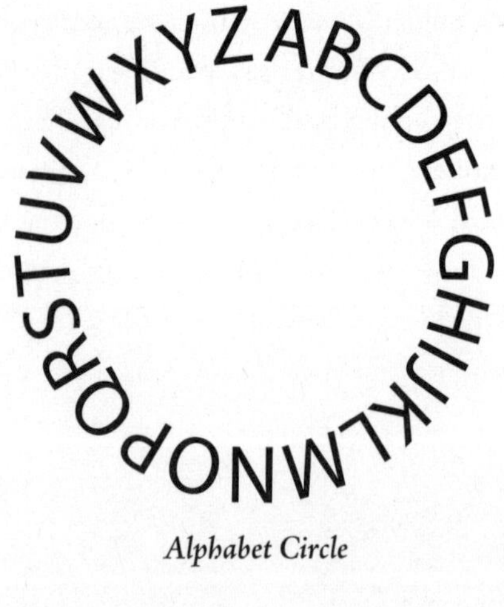

Alphabet Circle

Think of a one-word intention. Now take a pencil. Don't worry. I promise I won't tell anyone. Put it on the first letter of the intention. Draw a line to the second letter. And from the second to the third. And the third to the fourth. And so on, until you are finished. You've just made a sigil! One using a system you might not have seen before, but it is still a sigil! Every morning, I have used this to draw one word corresponding to my daily affirmation. This takes all the guesswork out of sigil making, so I can do it with little time and effort. I then carry it around on me, letting the affirmation sink in. The next morning, I can take it off in the shower and repeat. There are several similar, lesser-known sigil-making systems that are usable for this, such as planetary squares or sigil wheels. If you like making sigils, I highly recommend you look into them!

If you make a matrix tattoo, you will want to experiment with the design before you get it. Make sure you have the ability to use it in a satisfactory way. Take the honeycomb tattoo. If you are going to use it by coloring in the hexagons to make a picture, it will look grainy, even if the honeycombs are small. So, take a marker, trace some small hexagons on your arm, and try coloring in an easy intention, such as a heart for love or a clover for luck. Make sure it looks good enough that you can connect to it. If you were to get a tattoo based on the Web of Wyrd, trace one on a piece of paper, then try to make bindrunes. Are there too few lines for you to make a satisfactory bindrune? Are your bindrunes usually really complicated? Make sure that you have a design with enough lines to comfortably contain any of your bindrunes.

In my opinion, this is the most difficult type of tattoo to think up. I highly encourage you get creative, though, because in my opinion these are the coolest!

The Devotional

I hesitated on whether to include this type of tattoo here because its primary purpose is not necessarily for magick. It has the potential to be quite versatile, though.

Some of you have deities or spirits you call upon for all sorts of things. These might be your matron/patron deities with whom you've built enough of a bond to ask for a greater range of things than others would. These might be deities of magick, such as Hecate, Heka, and Oya. They could also be deities who govern a large number of areas, such as Isis. They don't even have to be deities. You might have a favorite dragon or gnome you turn to for everything. The point is, if these beings are versatile to you, they can be called upon for a variety of intentions. This makes them magickally versatile. If you are thinking you want to show your devotion to a particular being but also want a versatile tattoo and only have the money for one, you might get the devotional tattoo. You would then call upon this being using the tattoo for whatever magick you're doing.

Again, these tattoos aren't meant to be magickal tools. They are more a place for you to make prayers and petitions. However, you might be one of the people who believes that magick is a divine gift, not a science we have yet to understand. If that is you, try this tattoo idea on for size. Tattoo your deity and have them pointing to a person who has their arms up in front of them like they are holding something. The next time you want to work magick, draw what you want to bring to you in the arms of the person. That is a very poignant way to represent your deity giving you the opportunity (pointing at you) to bring to yourself whatever you want (your arms in front of you, capable of holding). Drawing your intention in the person's hands represents you exercising that power in spellwork.

Outstretched hands aren't the only way to represent you working the magick that is your divine gift, letting you use this kind of tattoo for devotion *and* spells. The deity could be pointing to you, and you could be pointing to a summoning triangle in the ground, where you will draw your intention. You can also create a devotional tattoo that is part you, part deity. Have them holding something in front of them but have the face be half them and half you or have them situated behind you, mirroring the gesture you are making. This would signify their power being the source of your power or you tapping into their power to bring something to you.

We're done with designing now. You know what your tattoo is going to look like, but not so fast! We aren't going into working magick while getting tattooed just yet. None of the steps to getting a tattoo are so unimportant they should be thrown in the back of the book, so we might as well go through them in order. Before you get tattooed, you need to be sure you're going to the right studio and at the right time. That is the next chapter.

8

The Set-Up: Finding an Artist and Timing the Tattoo

Now that you designed your new tattoo, it's time to get the ball rolling on getting to the tattoo session. The first step is finding a tattoo artist, especially one who is comfortable with tattoo magick. Some of you are lucky enough to have a good relationship with a Witch-friendly artist. The good news for everyone else is, outside of the Bible Belt, most tattoo shops are cool with Witches and Witch tattoos. A surprising number of tattoo artists are Witches, too. Two of my five tattoo artists are Witches or dabbled at some point. A third said he thought everyone was in some way Pagan. And I don't know for sure with the last two since it never came up. To be clear, many tattoo artists may be used to Witches and the tattoos Witches get. Actually participating in magick might be new, though. It might be a step too far for them. But by and large, it will not be too difficult to find the perfect person.

After you figure out who will do your tattoo, your second step in setting your tattoo up for success is figuring out when the appointment should happen. You, like me, might be a very spur-of-the-moment person when it comes to working magick. You might have a rigid, inflexible schedule, like my partner. For something as expensive as tattoos, for which there is finite space to put new ones, you might as well pull out all the stops to give your magick more oomph. Doesn't matter how spur-of-the-moment you like to be. If you can, take a look at timing.

Finding the Right Tattoo Artist

Let's get the elephant out of the room. You're looking for two things: someone who will be comfortable with tattoo magick, and someone who will do a good job. I've chosen to go over the second one first because it's arguably more important. I would rather get a tattoo done well and do the tattoo magick after it heals than do magick in the session with a tattoo I will regret forever. Don't worry, though; you will get both.

Portfolio

The easiest way to get some of the worse artists out of the way is to look for that artist's portfolio. Do this first. Frequently the tattoo shop's website will have photos of work by their artists, and the artists usually have social media accounts. When you find it, there are a few things you should be sure to look for in someone's portfolio:

Linework: The lines in the photos should have even thickness. When they need to be straight, they should be straight.

Detail: The artist should be able to pack in a fair amount of detail without the lines looking like they are going to bleed into each other.

Patches: For tattoos where there is a decent-sized patch of one color, the color should be consistent. Making sure the colors are even is very difficult, but necessary. If you consistently see color that looks patchy, the artist is not that good.

Realism: If you see a tattoo that looks like it might as well have been a photo, that's a sign of a good artist. Look for faces; those are more difficult.

Custom work: If all the tattoos look like photocopies of each other or stereotypical tattoos, that's a sign the artist is only using premade templates they feel comfortable with. A good tattoo artist should be able to cleanly execute a piece they have never done before. Their portfolio should have a lot of variety in their work. There should also be work that looks original or custom.

A variety of styles: Having a variety of styles in their portfolio is a good indicator of skill because usually they won't put it in their portfolio unless they are comfortable with showing it off. There is one exception: Many well-known tattoo artists exclusively do one style, and they do it extremely well. If they have more than fifteen thousand followers on their social media and only one style, then they do the style because they're well known for it.

Reviews

Every business has reviews. Look up the studio and search specifically for your artist's name. Don't just look for any comments on how good the tattoo is. Look for descriptions of how nice they were and how well they worked with their client to find the perfect tattoo.

And keep in mind that not every bad review is a sign of a bad artist; it might be a rotten reviewer. Balance bad reviews against the good.

Check Out the Shop

If an artist is meticulous about their work, they will be meticulous about other parts of the tattooing process. Go into the shop and look at how put together it is. The number one thing you should look for is cleanliness. This is technically a medical procedure, so sterility is of utmost importance. While you're there, check out how friendly the people are who are working there. You're not just paying for a good tattoo. You're paying for a good experience *especially if you are practicing magick during it.*

Experience Is Not Expertise

Louder for those in the back: Experience is not expertise! I had someone give me a tattoo while I was on vacation who had twenty years' experience. It was small and simple. He screwed that up royally. Meanwhile, I was shocked to find my current artist had only eight years of experience. This is a woman who did a detailed sleeve so well that two people commented on the linework in the first four months.

So, I will say it again: Experience is not expertise.

Finding Someone Witchy or Witch-Friendly

When it comes to practicing tattoo magick, provided you're doing magick in the tattoo session, you absolutely must tell your tattoo artist about it. Even if you aren't doing magick then, chances are high they'll know what they're tattooing before they start. A tattoo artist once told me that if he didn't know what something was, he would always ask, making sure he wasn't going to tattoo something he'd regret. I haven't met anyone to date who has said otherwise. All of this is to say: If you are going to be doing any sort of magick or getting a magickal-looking tattoo, you're going to want someone Witch-friendly. If nothing else, it will avoid any negative vibes during the session.

Word of mouth is one of the best ways to find a Witch-friendly tattoo artist. There are groups for everything on social media, including Witches in your state or county. Search for some, and post to them asking people where they got their tattoos done. Be sure to specify that you're looking for someone Witch-friendly because you will be working tattoo magick. If you want to work with a Witch, rather than someone Witch-friendly, be sure to specify. Alternatively, you could search online for Witchy tattoo artists in your area. Not all tattoo artists who are Witches are open about it, though. Keep that in mind. If you want to work with a Witch but there aren't any coming up on a search engine, you will have to do some digging. Find the social media profiles of artists in the area and look for anything in the description that would suggest they're a Witch—things such as moon emojis or the word "spiritual" or any mention of other Witch-adjacent professions, such as reiki practitioner. If in doubt, look at any photos of their work on social media and see if there are an unusual number that are Witchy or Witch-adjacent.

If your tattoo artist is a Witch, there is a chance they don't want you working magick during the session. Sometimes Witch tattoo artists have their own magickal practices during tattooing, and your spellwork *as you present it to them* might interfere. Either find someone else if you feel strongly about this or work to make some sort of magickal compromise.

What if you don't need to work with a Witch but do want someone Witch-friendly? Go find local tattoo shop websites and take a look at the photos. Are there several tattoo photos that are Witchy? Seeing the same symbol in multiple photos is especially a good sign.

Don't pay attention to runes, though. A lot of non-magickal people, such as my hair stylist, will get a single rune or words in runes.

If you find multiple tattoo shops with people who seem Witchy or Witch-friendly, it's time to talk to them. When I was looking for a new tattoo studio in the area I moved to, I narrowed the search to two and emailed both of them saying I liked the photos of people's work and wanted to know if anyone in the shop liked working on Witch-related tattoos. Only one responded; they said, "We all do." That was all I needed to know. I came in and gave the person who walked to the front desk my tattoo idea. He gave me a breakdown of the cost, how long it would take, and the size it would have to be. He set me up with Marilyn Charles for the following day (hey girl!!). One of the reasons for doing so was that my tattoo was very detailed, and Marilyn works *really* well with detail. Making sure you are matched with the right tattoo artist is a sign of a good tattoo studio. And it was a great match; I've used her for almost all of my tattoos since.

What to Ask and What to Say

I will repeat, if you are going to work tattoo magick, you have to let your tattoo artist know. But how do you go about that? And other than that, what do you say?

Here is a list of questions that would be very helpful to ask:

- How comfortable are you with applying tattoos on people that are related to Witchcraft?
    - They will say they are comfortable, but you should ask.
- Do you like making those tattoos?

- I was planning to work magick with this tattoo. Specifically, I wanted to do a spell for [intention] while you were tattooing me. Are you comfortable with that?
- Are you comfortable with me blessing the ink before you start?
- I was hoping to bring a couple things with me but wanted to know if there are any restrictions. For example, can I bring in some incense?[61]

Timing

Look, we've all gotten the itch to get a tattoo that we just don't want to wait for. If you're planning not to wait, great! Really. One of my biggest pieces was something I had planned for a while, but one day I just told myself I had to have it. The next day, I was getting it on me. I don't regret a single thing about it. But if you're willing to wait, or your tattoo artist is so good they have to be booked a while in advance, you can time it so the energies of the moment match well with your intention. I have four different ways by which you can time your tattoo: the phases of the moon, the moon sign, the day of the week, and the planetary hour.

The Phases of the Moon

As a Witch, it is somewhat likely you work with the phases of the moon in magick, at least at a basic level. The full moon is a time for all magickal endeavors. The new moon is for beginnings. The waxing moon is for bringing things toward you. The waning moon is for banishing and introspection. The phase of the moon can be further broken down, though, into quarters or even eighths. Each eighth has its own correspondences, which are in the table below. For this

---

61. Only a couple of things! Don't take advantage of a gracious host.

information I am very grateful to Silver RavenWolf, whose correspondences I wrote down twenty years ago. They worked so well for me they haven't changed much after all this time. If you get a chance, I highly recommend going out and getting a copy of her book *Solitary Witch*. It is full of more information than you could ever hope to learn.

Moon Phase Summary

Name	*Timing*	*Appearance*	*Magickal Uses*
New moon	Right at the moment of the new moon to ~3.5 days later		Beginnings, potential
Waxing crescent	~3.5 to 7 days after the new moon	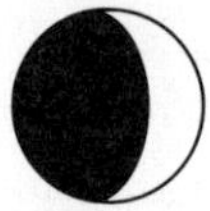	Action, motivation
First quarter moon	~7 to 10.5 days after the new moon	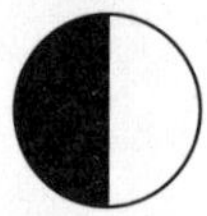	Building on a foundation, shaping the clay
Waxing gibbous	~10.5 to 14 days after the new moon	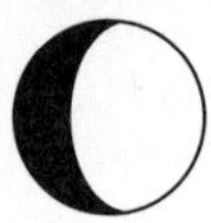	Refinement, personal growth
Full moon	~14 to 17.5 days after the new moon	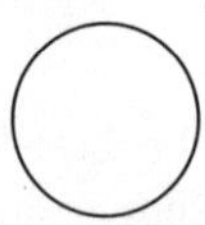	Completion, magick in general
Waning gibbous	~17.5 to 21 days after the new moon	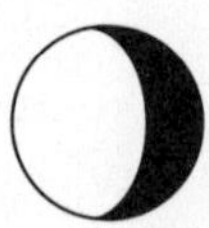	Knowledge, reflection

Name	*Timing*	*Appearance*	*Magickal Uses*
Last quarter moon	~21 to 24.5 days after the new moon	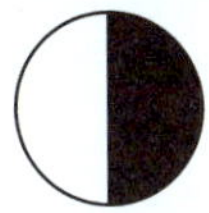	Destruction, banishing
Waning crescent	~24.5 to 28 days after the new moon	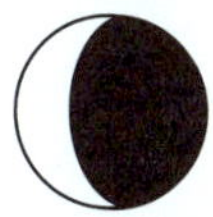	Divination and psychism

These correspondences, of course, are just guidelines. If you have always associated a particular moon phase with something else, go with that. I, for example, associate the new moon with magick in general, not the full moon. But, since I'm not most people, I kept "magick in general" with the full moon for you all. Whichever association you make is the right one for you.

The Moon Sign

For any of you magickal practitioners who don't know a thing about astrology, ancient astrologers divided the night sky according to twelve constellations: Aries, Taurus, Gemini, and so on. Each constellation is associated with certain characteristics: Taurus with stability; Leo with creativity; Gemini with intelligence. When a heavenly body passes through that sign, it is a signal of what energies will show up in the part of life that body governs in astrology. This includes the sun. The sign it was in when you were born is what you answer to when people ask you "What's your sign?" This also includes, importantly for us, the moon.

The moon rules, among other things, intuition and magick. Therefore the sign the moon is in will, according to astrology, influence which types of magick will work best. Truly, you can time your magick using any heavenly body depending on your intention. If you are working a love spell, for example, you might want to pay special attention to the sign Venus is in. But the moon has special influence over magick and, luckily for us, changes sign approximately every two and a half days, making it much easier to time our works according to the moon than another body.

Below is a table with the moon sign and the types of intentions that sign is good for.

Moon Sign Correspondences

Moon Sign	*Correspondences*
Aries	Initiative, leadership, authority, willpower, competition
Taurus	Prosperity, endurance, love, home life, stability
Gemini	Communication, writing, travel, friends, flexibility
Cancer	Home life, health, getting in touch with your feelings
Leo	Authority, courage, fertility, love, creativity
Virgo	Employment, health, organization, finding truth
Libra	Balance, justice, partnerships, karma, peace
Scorpio	Transformation, psychism, sex, banishing, protection
Sagittarius	Experimentation, adventure, travel, legal matters
Capricorn	Discipline, career, success, ambition, banishing
Aquarius	Self-expression, friendship, creativity
Pisces	Dreams, psychism, emotion work, introspection

If you are going to use this system of timing—and you don't have to; this is more to give your magick an extra oomph—you're going to need to know what sign the moon will be in at a given time. If you search "moon calendar," you'll find some websites that have entries for what sign the moon will be in on any given day. If it is transitioning from one sign to another, you will see the time of that transition. You can also consult a magickal almanac, which will have calendar pages with that information. I will repeat that it only takes about two and a half days for the moon to change signs. There are twelve signs. Even if you just missed the right sign, you only need to wait a month to be back in the perfect place. And for something that will be a permanent part of your body, if you already were patient enough to think through timing, a month will not be that long.

There is a chance, if you look up what sign the moon is in now, you will see something saying the moon is "void of course." That means the moon has no more meaningful astrological interactions between it and the other planets before it enters a new sign. This can last anywhere from a few minutes to several hours. For some Witches, casting magick when the moon is void of course is bad news. If the moon is void of course, there isn't much focus to the magick, so it is best done another day. Whether you choose to follow this belief is up to what feels right for you. If it's important, though, you should definitely keep an eye out for this.

The Day of the Week

Each day of the week has traditionally been associated with one of the seven classical "planets": Mercury, Venus, Mars, Jupiter, Saturn, the sun, and the moon. Because of that, each day is associated with the particular energies of that planet. While many people will wait until the weekend to get their tattoo, tattoo studios are frequently open late on weekdays. If you aren't working sixteen-hour days, five days per week, I would recommend choosing a day that aligns with your intention. The table below shows you the energies of each day. Please keep in mind not every tattoo studio is open every day of the week.

Day of the Week Correspondences

Day	*Planet*	*Correspondences*
Sunday	Sun	Success, power, authority, loyalty
Monday	Moon	Psychism, intuition, emotion, creativity, home life
Tuesday	Mars	Action, aggression, protection, strategy, courage
Wednesday	Mercury	Intellect, communication, flexibility
Thursday	Jupiter	Expansion, money, growth, luck
Friday	Venus	Love, self-care, creativity
Saturday	Saturn	Banishing, discipline, protection, justice, career success

The Planetary Hours

Here we get into a rather esoteric branch of magickal timing. It was more popular back when magickal systems leaned more heavily on ceremonial systems. Of all the methods of timing, it is both the most convenient—because you cycle through these energies multiple times per day—and the most confusing—because planetary hours last such a short time. Just as planetary energies cycle through each day of the week, with one energy predominant each day, so do they, to a lesser extent, cycle regularly throughout the day. There are twelve planetary "hours" between sunrise and sunset and twelve planetary "hours" between sunset and the following sunrise. Which hour corresponds to which planet's energy depends on the day. There is a table below that shows the sequence of hours.

Daytime Planetary Hours

	Sunday	*Monday*	*Tuesday*	*Wednesday*	*Thursday*	*Friday*	*Saturday*
Hour 1 (sunrise)	Sun	Moon	Mars	Mercury	Jupiter	Venus	Saturn
Hour 2	Venus	Saturn	Sun	Moon	Mars	Mercury	Jupiter
Hour 3	Mercury	Jupiter	Venus	Saturn	Sun	Moon	Mars
Hour 4	Moon	Mars	Mercury	Jupiter	Venus	Saturn	Sun
Hour 5	Saturn	Sun	Moon	Mars	Mercury	Jupiter	Venus
Hour 6	Jupiter	Venus	Saturn	Sun	Moon	Mars	Mercury
Hour 7	Mars	Mercury	Jupiter	Venus	Saturn	Sun	Moon
Hour 8	Sun	Moon	Mars	Mercury	Jupiter	Venus	Saturn
Hour 9	Venus	Saturn	Sun	Moon	Mars	Mercury	Jupiter
Hour 10	Mercury	Jupiter	Venus	Saturn	Sun	Moon	Mars
Hour 11	Moon	Mars	Mercury	Jupiter	Venus	Saturn	Sun
Hour 12	Saturn	Sun	Moon	Mars	Mercury	Jupiter	Venus

Nighttime Planetary Hours

	Sunday	*Monday*	*Tuesday*	*Wednesday*	*Thursday*	*Friday*	*Saturday*
Hour 1 (sunset)	Jupiter	Venus	Saturn	Sun	Moon	Mars	Mercury
Hour 2	Mars	Mercury	Jupiter	Venus	Saturn	Sun	Moon
Hour 3	Sun	Moon	Mars	Mercury	Jupiter	Venus	Saturn
Hour 4	Venus	Saturn	Sun	Moon	Mars	Mercury	Jupiter
Hour 5	Mercury	Jupiter	Venus	Saturn	Sun	Moon	Mars
Hour 6	Moon	Mars	Mercury	Jupiter	Venus	Saturn	Sun
Hour 7	Saturn	Sun	Moon	Mars	Mercury	Jupiter	Venus
Hour 8	Jupiter	Venus	Saturn	Sun	Moon	Mars	Mercury
Hour 9	Mars	Mercury	Jupiter	Venus	Saturn	Sun	Moon
Hour 10	Sun	Moon	Mars	Mercury	Jupiter	Venus	Saturn
Hour 11	Venus	Saturn	Sun	Moon	Mars	Mercury	Jupiter
Hour 12	Mercury	Jupiter	Venus	Saturn	Sun	Moon	Mars

I wish I could say this was as easy as Planet A rules from five to six in the morning, Planet B rules from six to seven in the morning, and so on. But remember that there are twelve hours between sunrise and sunset. The planetary "hours" would only be one hour long if there were exactly twelve hours between sunrise and sunset. If there were nine hours of daylight, each daytime planetary hour would be only forty-five minutes long. If there were fifteen hours of daylight, a planetary hour would be seventy-five minutes long.

Calculating the planetary hours for a given day is very involved, requiring the above tables with the sunrise and sunset times of a given day and the sunrise time of the following day. You also need a little math. Luckily, we live in the age of the computer. Just search "planetary hours calculator." You'll find websites that will give you the planetary hours for a given date and location. Super handy, super easy. If you were to look up planetary hours for April 14, 2025, where I live, you would find the information shared on the opposite page.

Planetary Hours on April 14, 2025

Hour	*Start*	*Stop*	*Planet*
1	6:25 a.m.	7:31 a.m.	Moon
2	7:31 a.m.	8:37 a.m.	Saturn
3	8:37 a.m.	9:43 a.m.	Jupiter
4	9:43 a.m.	10:49 a.m.	Mars
5	10:49 a.m.	11:55 a.m.	Sun
6	11:55 a.m.	1:01 p.m.	Venus
7	1:01 p.m.	2:07 p.m.	Mercury
8	2:07 p.m.	3:13 p.m.	Moon
9	3:13 p.m.	4:19 p.m.	Saturn
10	4:19 p.m.	5:25 p.m.	Jupiter
11	5:25 p.m.	6:31 p.m.	Mars
12	6:31 p.m.	7:37 p.m.	Sun

Hour	*Start*	*Stop*	*Planet*
1	7:37 p.m.	8:31 p.m.	Venus
2	8:31 p.m.	9:25 p.m.	Mercury
3	9:25 p.m.	10:18 p.m.	Moon
4	10:18 p.m.	11:12 p.m.	Saturn
5	11:12 p.m.	12:06 a.m.	Jupiter
6	12:06 a.m.	1:00 a.m.	Mars
7	1:00 a.m.	1:54 a.m.	Sun
8	1:54 a.m.	2:48 a.m.	Venus
9	2:48 a.m.	3:42 a.m.	Mercury
10	3:42 a.m.	4:36 a.m.	Moon
11	4:36 a.m.	5:29 a.m.	Saturn
12	5:29 a.m.	6:23 a.m.	Jupiter

If I had a tattoo appointment on April fourteenth of this year, starting at six in the evening, it would fall under the eleventh hour, ruled by Mars. I might decide to get a tattoo then for clear-sightedness in a fraught situation, protection from people who wish me harm, or motivation for self-improvement. If we had to move the tattoo back to ten that night, that would be the hour of the moon. I might instead get a tattoo to enhance psychic abilities or calm my hotheadedness. You know. If I were awake then.

Now, I know some of you are thinking, "But Jake, there is no way my artist can get my tattoo done in that little time. Won't it mess things up if the tattoo crosses multiple planetary hours?" Keep in mind that you almost certainly won't be raising energy the entire time you are being tattooed. I think for me it is ten to fifteen minutes on average, so my guess is you'll usually be done in the first half hour. If you are still worried, though, as long as you start in the appropriate planetary hour, you'll be fine. That ensures you have the right energies to propel yourself and your intention forward. And please keep in mind, magickal timing doesn't really work against you; it works to magnify your power.

The final thing I will say about planetary hours, given they can sometimes be quite short, is to keep in mind your tattoo artist might wait until you arrive before starting to set up. The time it takes to set up can vary quite a bit, so you might want to ask your tattoo artist ahead of time approximately how long they think this will take so you can plan to start within the planetary hour you want.

Examples of Magickal Timing

This was a very long section! The topic is worth all the attention it gets, though. For many people, timing is a crucial component. Truly, though, if you don't think magickal timing is important, or are getting a tattoo last minute, you don't have to follow it. Again, I encourage you to think of the timing as giving an added boost.

I figured I would close with a couple examples to pull it all together. These vary in complexity, because timing can be as simple or as complex as you want.

Example #1: A Heartbreak Tattoo

James just got dumped by his partner and is really torn up about it. He's no longer actively crying, but he still feels quite vulnerable. He isn't sure he is strong enough to put himself out there again. He is also feeling very bitter, which he knows isn't an accurate assessment of the years he spent with his partner. He knows that if he allows the bitterness to take hold, it could affect future relationships. He would like to get a tattoo to help him heal from the breakup, to banish the negative emotions and leave the good things from the relationship. More importantly, he wants a reminder that there is always good in putting himself out there and seeking love. Because he wanted the constant reminder, he was always going to get a tattoo. Working spells with the tattoo is getting two things done at once. Efficiency!

He doesn't want his negativity to fester, so he goes to his tattoo studio at once. The owner of the studio says they have someone available that evening if he wants. He checks and sees today is the full moon. He knows this tattoo would work best with banishing energies, so he asks the owner if there's an opening tomorrow, when the moon starts to wane. The owner books him for one in the afternoon.

Example #2: A Success Nexus

Emily wants a tattoo to supercharge her career. She has lofty business goals for the next three to five years at her company and wants to set herself up for success. This is a spell she wants to get right, and considering how ambitious she is, she wants maximal power on her side.

Since it's for a three-to-five-year goal, she feels she can wait for the perfect time. She consults her charts, coming to the conclusion that she will want to do this close to noon since that is the time of abundance. She sees Taurus is associated with luxury and Capricorn with success. Jupiter is associated with abundance, and the sun with success. She'll want some combination of Capricorn, Taurus, Jupiter, and sun energies, so she does some looking. Thursday is associated with Jupiter and Sunday with the sun. On Sundays, Jupiter rules one of the planetary hours that most often is close to, but after, noon. That works for her because her tattoo studio never opens before noon, and her tattoo artist would need a half hour to set up. She also is busy during the week, so Thursday would not be ideal. This combines time of day, day of week, and planetary hour in a rather comprehensive way.

Emily gets a lot of abundance and success energies already, but she wants to throw in some moon timing. This way she can bring in some of the energies of Taurus or Capricorn. She does want to be sure, whenever it is, that the moon is waxing so she can bring things to her. She starts looking for a Sunday when the moon is waxing and in the sign of Capricorn or Taurus. She finds a date in January when the moon is in Taurus.

Unfortunately, that is four months out. She thinks she's fine with that, but her artist only books appointments so far out. She texts her usual artist to ask how far in advance she does bookings. The artist tells her that normally it's only two months out and she can't be sure she'll be available that far in advance. When told the date, the artist chuckles and says Emily is lucky. That date is right after a big annual family vacation, and she always works overtime afterward to pay for all the money she spends. She happily pencils Emily in.

Now with all of that, there is nothing left before you go in and get the tattoo itself. So, let's talk about the tattoo session. We'll start with the bit I know you are most interested in: how to work magick during it.

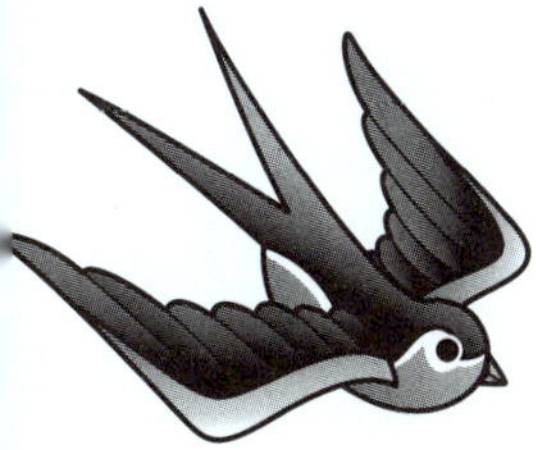

9
Making Magick in the Tattooing Session

At the beginning of this book, I told you many ways you could use your healed tattoos for magick. But that's not the full extent of it. As I've mentioned, you can work magick during the tattooing session itself, especially when the tattoo you are getting greatly reflects your intention. Think about it. Magick operates best on symbols. Well, in the tattoo session, you are literally creating the thing that is your outcome. What better symbolic parallel is there? There are also some great methods of raising energy associated with tattooing, including utilizing the pain. You combine energy raising and a symbol/visualization to direct the energy, and you have magick!

More on the Parts of Magick in a Tattoo Session

Now, what I just described was a very simplified, bare-bones description of tattoo magick. In this section, I'll dive a little deeper into the different components of spellwork and how you would work with them in the tattooing session.

Visualization

This is the lowest hanging fruit in tattoo session magick: The best visualization to use in your tattoo session is the tattoo you are getting. Well gee, ain't that handy?

Now, frequently the visualization is in your mind. That's kind of the definition of "visualization." But some of you might be a step ahead of me and thinking, "Well, in the tattoo session, they're making my tattoo. Can't I just focus on that? Wouldn't that actually be a very poignant symbol of my intention coming to life?" Yes, you can do that! But! I don't advise it for everyone. I find it to be a little distracting watching the tattoo being applied, if I'm not raising energy with pain. It's harder to have the pain become something in the back of your mind if you're watching it happen, which makes it more difficult to feel and raise energy. Now, there are some people who find it natural to feel energy, without thinking about it. It's second nature to them. For those people, sure, they can watch the tattoo being made to focus on the spell. For the rest of us, it's probably better to keep the visualization in your mind if you aren't raising energy with pain.

Visualization can be difficult, much more so the more complicated the image is. If the tattoo is overly complicated, then, wouldn't that hinder your visualization? Yes and no. First, if you think the tattoo is too complicated to visualize, simplify the visualization! Remember reading about how to simplify your tattoo in chapter 2? It is very doable. Second, if we try to visualize something complicated, our brains naturally simplify the image to the most detailed version we can get. So, the work is done for us. That's riskier, though, because sometimes you'll screen out some of the important bits. But it is done for you. The real issue is if you go into it thinking, "Oh, this is too complicated. Oh, this is too complicated." Because then you psych yourself out.

Raising Energy

Raising energy is a key component of spellwork, whether you are conscious of doing it or not. Do you ever feel the vibes shift as you chant? Do you find you tighten up just slightly right before the spell is finished? Does the air feel different after a spell? Warmer, perhaps? Those are signs of energy being raised and released. If raising energy is not a key part of your practice, I highly recommend the book *Magical Power for Beginners* by Deborah Lipp. You'll find it transforms your practice, for the better.

While some people may argue deliberate energy raising isn't necessary for magick, it sure as hell makes it feel more effective. If you don't deliberately raise energy, I'd request you do a little experiment. Let's find a set of circumstances where you do magick enough that you instinctively know how it feels to work magick then. Perhaps there is a type of magick you do more frequently or a time you do it more frequently. The next time you are in those circumstances, after you've lit the candle or burned the petition or finished making the poppet, pick up a rattle. You don't have to go out and buy one. Just grab a saltshaker or a small container half filled with rice. Bring the visualization you decided on into your head and start shaking the rattle. Shake at what you feel is a normal pace. After a little bit, you may feel the shaking start to speed up. Allow it. Go with it. Let it continue to slowly speed up until it is at the fastest speed possible. When it is at maximum speed, continue to shake for a few seconds more ... and then stop. Release the visualization. The spell is done.

How did that feel? What sensations are going through you? Perhaps there's a tension or release in the air? How do you feel about the spell you cast? Did it feel powerful? How quickly do you think it will come to fruition? I'm willing to bet nine out of ten times of you will come from your spell feeling more powerful, and more confident in the outcome, now that you experienced firsthand the process of raising and sending energy.

There are several ways to raise energy during the tattoo session. Regarding all of these techniques, I'm going to suggest you not use the "typical" method of raising and sending energy, which is to continue building energy until there is a peak, then send it. There is another method of raising energy that Lipp calls "female power sending" in her book *Magical Power for Beginners,* partially because the cadence is similar to a female orgasm (as a gay man, I'll take her word on it). Build up little bits of energy, then release them, over and over, until you either cannot send any more or feel enough has been sent.

This method of energy raising works *perfectly* for tattooing. Your tattoo artist needs to stop every several seconds to do things such as refill the ink or move to a different spot. It may take a few seconds for them to get back at it, and it's difficult to hold on to or continue raising energy if the thing you've been using to work with it has suddenly vanished and you don't know when it's coming back again. So, use the time when the tattoo is being drawn on you to raise energy. When the artist pulls away, release the energy. Start raising when they get back at it again. Release when they pull away. Repeat. Provided the tattoo doesn't take thirty seconds, you'll send out all you need when they finish.

Of the methods of raising energy during your session, one is pain, which you'll read about more in the next chapter. Pain has some very powerful links to spiritual experiences, making it potent as a method of raising energy if you are comfortable with it. However, pain is not the only way to raise power. In fact, it isn't even that good of a way when the tattoo you're getting doesn't hurt very much. What wave can you ride when you're in a kiddie pool? If you don't think pain will be the route to go, I suggest using the vibration from the tattoo needle. The needle isn't vibrating, it's puncturing your skin, but it does it so quickly and rhythmically that it feels like a buzzing or vibration on your skin.

People who are squeamish about pain might find this method of energy raising very helpful. I've actually found that by actively focusing on the vibrations, tattoos hurt less. Not just less in energy raising, less in general! It may seem counterintuitive, because the vibrations are where the hurting happens, but my leading theory is that you're actively focusing on something else so you can't focus on the pain. It's just easier to focus on that than, say, your breath, because the vibrations make for a very powerful, unusual sensation.

Some people believe that magick works because all things in this Universe vibrate at certain frequencies. Since like attracts like, magick works by changing your vibration to match that of what you want to bring to you. For those people, this method of raising power is thus both intuitive and poetic. The act of being tattooed is you using vibrations to change your spiritual vibration. If this is your belief, this is the method that will be most powerful for you. For anyone else, go with what makes sense for you. You can decide that ahead of time or test out both methods in the first few minutes of the tattoo. Whichever is helping you connect better, go with that.

Energy-Raising Technique: Vibration

I want you to feel the vibrations on your skin from the tattoo needle. I want you to feel the movement, the tingling spreading away from the tattoo site. Every breath you take, you feel more of your body vibrating with the tattoo needle. When the tattoo needle leaves your body, the vibrations die down somewhat, but not all the way. When the needle goes back in you, they kick up again. Your body is rippling, pulsing with the sympathetic energies of the tattoo needle, matching your intention, bringing it closer to you. Your body is now sensitized to the vibration you need. When the tattoo needle is removed, the vibrations die; when it goes back in you, it is like they never left. The next time the tattoo needle comes to your skin, I want you to bring the visualization to your mind and keep it there. Feel the outcome you are striving for. Know that every moment of sympathetic vibration generates energy you can use to bring your outcome to you. Every time you send your energy, you affirm the frequency at which you are vibrating. Every time you send your energy, it is a signal to the Universe that this is yours, you deserve this, it *will* come to you. Now, feel the energy when the tattoo needle is brought down to your skin. Feel the vibrations, and then send to your outcome when the needle is moved away. Feel the vibrations when it is brought back to your skin, raise them, and send out when it moves away. Continue with this cycle until you feel it's enough or that you can't raise energy anymore.

Putting It Together

Okay, so to put it all together: While the tattooing happens, bring a visual of your outcome or of your completed tattoo to your mind, and raise energy from the pain or the vibrations. It is best not to raise energy to a peak and then release, but to raise energy when the needle is in you and release what you've raised when the needle is taken away. Repeat when the needle starts going through your skin again.

Improving Your Tattoo Session Magick

There are so many ways you can get creative with tattooing magick and so many things you can do to enhance the energy and likelihood of success. Take these suggestions just as a jumping-off point.

Charging the Ink

The ink is extremely important. It is what is going inside you and giving form to your tattoo. Of course all magick works with unseen energy, but that doesn't mean you don't need to bless your tools before you start working. If you do one thing from this list of tips, it should be charging the ink with your intention.

As with everything else in this section, you can make this as complicated or as simple as you want. Keep in mind, though, that it's your tattoo artist who will be dealing with the ink, not you. Don't do anything that would get in their way or prevent them from giving you the best tattoo they can. Avoid complicated movements that make it more likely you'll accidentally spill. Don't take thirty minutes—unless you want to pay your artist for thirty minutes of their time.

Above all, *make sure your tattoo artist knows what you are doing ahead of time.* They are handling the ink directly. If they are even the slightest bit uncomfortable with magick, this can feel like a violation. The markings you make on your skin, the crystals you're holding, the clothing you're wearing... that's all on your body. That's your thing. The ink is their thing.

To charge the inks, look at the ink cups. Imagine an invisible dome on the tray that contains the inks safely within it. In your head, say,

For the magickal working I am undertaking,
These sacred inks I hereby charge.
As they enter my body,
May their energies enter my life.
As they settle in my body,
May their energies settle into place,
Bringing [intention] *into my life.*

Bring the visualization of your intent to your mind.

On inhales through your nose, bring energy into your body from the air around you. It moves throughout your body, being infused with your intention. Exhale through your mouth, seeing the energies firing like a beam of light toward the inks. As they enter the invisible dome, they scatter, spreading throughout it. By the fourth exhale, the dome is almost thrumming with energy. It can barely contain any more. There is nothing more the dome can contain after the fifth breath. There is more energy than you thought possible. On a final, sixth exhale, see the energy being sucked into the cup or cups until there is nothing left. Trace an equal-armed cross in the air with your finger to seal the energies.

Adding Correspondences

As you know, the more correspondences you use in magick, up to a point, the more powerful it will be, so you can incorporate correspondences in the tattooing session to bring your intention to fruition faster. The first place you could incorporate correspondences is your clothes. The easiest way to do that is with color. Refer to the below table for color correspondences. When you find a matching color, see if you have any casual clothes that are that color. This doesn't mean you have to be that color head to toe, looking like a blueberry or something. Prioritize clothing that you will keep on during the tattoo appointment and clothing that is close to the tattoo site. That way, if you look at the artist doing their work, you'll see the color more often. If you have no clothes in that color, go out to a less-expensive clothing store and buy a T-shirt. Alternatively, get your nails painted that color (guys, you too).

Color Correspondences

Color	*Correspondences*
Red	Passion, lust, action, war, strength
Orange	Courage, opportunities, breaking blockages, happiness, success
Yellow	Happiness, success, self-esteem, communication
Green	Healing, nature, prosperity, hope
Blue	Healing, peace, emotions, meditation
Purple	Wisdom, spirituality, devotion
Pink	Love, being carefree, friendship, harmony
White	Cleansing, spirituality, communication, health, all-purpose
Black	Banishing, protection, discipline, all-purpose
Brown	Emotional regulation, security, support, nature
Silver	Psychism, spirituality, cycles, balance, illusion
Gold	Success, prosperity

Second, you could utilize crystal correspondences. This might be in the form of jewelry; many of us have rings with crystals embedded in them. You can also carry some crystals around in your pockets or a bag. Palm stones would be great because you can rub on them while getting tattooed. Really, though, any rock would be good. Speaking of jewelry, metals also have correspondences that may match your intention. Below are the correspondences for the more common metals and crystals.

Crystal and Metal Correspondences

Crystal/Metal	*Correspondences*
Amber	Stability, balance, beauty, longevity
Amethyst	Love, spirituality, spiritual connections, inspiration
Bloodstone	Abundance, vitality, conflict, overcoming obstacles
Carnelian	Communication, passion, focus, power
Citrine	Abundance, happiness, balance
Hematite	Banishing, protection, grounding, balance
Jade	Abundance, fertility
Labradorite	Spirituality, intuition, transformation
Lapis lazuli	Calm, healing heartbreak, love
Moonstone	Spirituality, intuition, emotional balance
Obsidian	Protection, banishing, focus
Clear quartz	All-purpose
Rose quartz	Love, comfort, healing, inner peace
Tiger's eye	Communication, confidence, empowerment
Brass	Healing, security
Copper	Love, creativity, fertility
Silver	Psychism, spirituality, cycles, balance, illusion
Gold	Success, prosperity

Smell is one of the most powerful senses we have. It has a stronger effect on memory and the subconscious than any other sense. If you have a collection of essential oils, you could take a look at their correspondences back in chapter 3 and see if there are any that match the intention for your tattoo. If the correspondences come from someone else, always double-check for yourself, because you make particularly strong associations with scent. Inhale the scent of the oil deeply, and ask yourself what thoughts come up. Do you get any impressions, memories, or images that match an intention? If you find there is an oil that smells like the intention you are going for, right before the tattoo session starts, put a couple drops on your neck where you feel your pulse and behind your ear.

Don't apply essential oils directly under your nostrils because that can be way too strong. That includes sniffing it from the bottle. I once sniffed peppermint essential oil as part of a calming ritual. I didn't realize it was too close to my skin until I felt a tingling on it … a very cold, intense tingling … which was traveling inside my nose. For the next three minutes, I was all but trying to inhale water from the faucet, trying to wash the oil off me. So, be sensible. As I've also said before, no cinnamon oil and very much avoid citrus oils. No more than three drops citrus in one ounce jojoba oil.

You may have noticed I've been covering the senses with these correspondences. Colors correspond to sight; crystals, especially the palm stones, correspond to touch; and essential oils correspond to smell. Whether it's correspondences or visualizations, the more senses you use, the better. Taste is rather hard. You could possibly suck on some hard candy in a flavor that corresponds to your intention, but that can draw your attention away. People make jokes about not being able to walk and chew gum at the same time; try doing magick and chewing gum at the same time. Hearing is an easy one: Make a playlist! The key, but also the tricky part, is to choose songs that aren't distracting. You don't want to be humming along to your favorite songs only to find that the tattoo is almost done! You also don't want to be trying to visualize and raise energy when suddenly that song you like comes on, and as hard as you try to focus, you can feel your attention being pulled away. Try to stick to music without lyrics or music that you played so much that now all the joy you've had is taken out of it.

There is one final way of incorporating correspondences, which is my personal favorite: drawing on yourself. You can't cover the tattoo area with marker. But the surrounding skin is fine! I like to fill the nearby area with sigils. The sigils could correspond to your intention. They could also represent the sacred entities you are calling upon during the ritual or be sigils of power in general. If you don't want to get fancy with sigils, you could just pepper shapes around the tattoo area, such as putting hearts everywhere for a self-love tattoo or drawing stars for an intuition enhancement.

If you are planning to draw around the tattoo, please keep in mind your tattoo artist is going to be using a fair amount of fluids as they tattoo you. Any markings around the tattoo are going to get smudged. So, either decide you don't care and that it won't distract you or use permanent marker. Add your drawings after the tattoo is placed, in case you decide to put it somewhere else.

Adding Witch Hazel to the Ink

Many tattoo artists will use witch hazel to dilute their ink and create different shades. It has the added benefit of helping with swelling and bleeding. It also happens to be a plant with quite a few correspondences. It can be used for banishing, healing, protection, wisdom, learning, love, psychism, and Witchcraft in general. Basically all-purpose! If you want a little Witchy flair, you can ask your tattoo artist to use a little witch hazel in the inks to help a little bit as you charge the ink. If you really prefer only black-and-white, ask your artist to put in just a couple drops. That's what my tattoo artist does, and really, you can't tell the difference.

Does that mean you should bring in herbs, tinctures, and oils, asking your artist to put them in the ink? Absolutely not. The witch hazel that artists use is sterile. Your items are not. It would be a bad idea for your artist to put them in the ink cup. Not to mention, if you brought in herbs, even if you ground them to a fine powder, they almost certainly will sink to the bottom of the cup and you'll get none of it in you. But that's okay, because witch hazel is basically all-purpose.

* · · · *

I did say in this chapter that using the pain to raise energy is a really cool and powerful idea. It deserves its own chapter, though, because there is a lot to talk about! Raising energy with pain isn't just a fun, creative thing that I can include to have you all say, "Oh, I think that's cool, so I like you a little more and may buy your next book maybe." There are a lot of links between pain and spiritual experiences, which gives pain a lot of special power as a method of making magick. And while you might take my word at it, I do want to show you more in depth where those links are and how we know. I do this especially for the people who are squeamish about the pain. If I can convince even one of you that the pain is a good thing, then you will relax more during your appointment and make it more likely that your magick will be fruitful. So, let's give it a fuller treatment. While I'm at it, I'll make a quick detour and tell those who are interested how they can work pain into other magick or meditations.

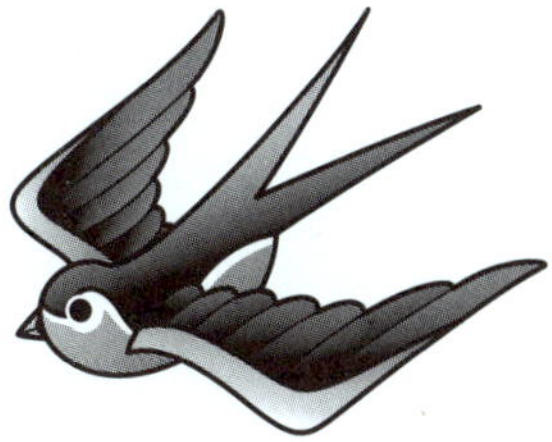

10
The Power in Pain

***Note:** In writing this chapter, I am not condoning self-harm. There is a big difference between harming oneself to manage emotional pain or compulsions and experiencing pain to achieve union with the Divine. Outside of tattooing, I do not advocate for any practice in this chapter that leads to irreversible marks on the body. If you yourself practice self-harm, I am sorry for the experiences that led you to that habit. I acknowledge your pain and the aspects of self-harm that perpetuate the behavior. I would sincerely request, however, that you try reaching out for help, whether it is to a trusted friend or a friendly, anonymous hotline.*

For those of you who haven't gotten a tattoo before, let me be plain: They hurt. Anyone who says tattoos don't hurt is lying to you. Some hurt differently depending on several factors, such as where you're being tattooed, how thick the needle is, and how much fat you have in your body. But they all hurt. It's a big reason people don't get tattoos, and for some of you, it might be the reason you're not so sure tattoo magick is for you. Really, magick should be for positive outcomes, and how can you focus on positive outcomes when you're in pain? Worse yet, will the spell turn out badly because your intention is being associated with something you really don't like?

I totally hear you on that. But what if I told you that pain could actually be used to good effect in magick? In other words: What if I told you that there is power in pain? I'll start by showing the connection between pain and spiritual experiences, as I believe this will provide a good foundation for you to be comfortable with this as a concept. I'll give techniques to help you channel this power during the appointment. Finally, there will be some exercises for you to practice raising energy with pain before your session. You want to make sure you're prepared, after all. For those who are interested, I'll show you how you can use those exercises to work with pain in magick and meditation more broadly.

The Intersection of Pain and Spirituality

If you look, you will find sanctioned practices of pain as part of most religions, even if you have to look into the past or into small sects of the religion. Some of you, I'm sure, immediately thought of self-flagellation. Self-flagellation—hitting oneself with whips or chains or something else to cause pain—has a history in Christianity.[62] It was certainly more prevalent centuries ago, but it still is practiced today by some. Even Pope John Paul II allegedly practiced it.[63] Self-flagellation has also been practiced by some communities of Shia Muslims and some Jews on the night before Yom Kippur.[64]

Fasting (which you should absolutely not do while getting a tattoo) is still a prominent pain practice in the monotheistic religions, on holidays such as Yom Kippur and the month of Ramadan. I rec-

62. Bertram, *Flagellation & the Flagellants*, 6–11; Vandermeersch, "Self-Flagellation in the Early Modern Era," 261–66.

63. Cirillo, "Self-Flagellation as Sanctification in the Roman Catholic Church's Prelature of the Holy Cross and Opus Dei," 10.

64. Scharbrodt, "Contesting Ritual Practices in Twelver Shiism," 1067; Rubel, "The Feast at the End of the Fast," 116.

ognize classifying fasting as pain/self-harm will be controversial, but people who have skipped a meal or two will tell you about the stomach cramping that can sometimes occur. While tips might be given to minimize these cramps, Islamic practitioners at least must still power through.[65] Ritual fasting is also a part of Buddhism and Hinduism.[66] The Sun Dance, a ritual performed by multiple Native American tribes, can also incorporate fasting.[67]

Multiple Hindu festivals or rituals and at least two Native American ceremonies incorporate the piercing of the body with skewers. Sometimes, people will attach heavy objects to the other ends of the skewers and pull those things behind them. A famous example is the Hindu festival of Thaipusam.[68] This is practiced not only in India but in various parts of Southeast Asia. The aforementioned Sun Dance, in North America, can incorporate the piercing of the body with skewers and dragging of heavy objects.[69] This is done as a spiritual offering, showing one's devotion to the community. There are even rituals in which the skewers are used to suspend oneself in midair. People do this as part of the Hindu Gajan festival to Shiva in India.[70] The Okipa ceremony, which used to be performed by Native Americans in the Dakotas, also incorporated ritual suspension.[71]

Prolonged walking barefoot is a component of several religious pilgrimages. Christians will climb one of Ireland's holiest mountains,

---

65. Siloam Hospitals Medical Team, "Causes and Treatments of Abdominal Pain During Fasting."

66. Islam, "Fasting in Hinduism, Buddhism and Islam," 25–30.

67. Spier, *The Sun Dance of the Plains Indians*, 477.

68. Ward, "Thaipusam in Malaysia," 307.

69. Spier, *The Sun Dance of the Plains Indians*, 462.

70. Dutta, "'Becoming Someone Else,'" 35.

71. Rada, "Extremely Up-In-The-Air," 96.

Croagh Patrick, barefoot as an act of penance.[72] There are portions of the Muslim pilgrimage to Mecca in Saudi Arabia where practitioners will walk barefoot as a mark of respect and devotion. Injuries are common.[73] Over in India, tens of thousands of Hindu men will perform a yearly pilgrimage, up to thirty-seven miles and up a mountain, to the Sabarimala temple. Traditionally, this pilgrimage is all done barefoot as a sign of spiritual devotion and to prepare the body for spiritual awakening. It frequently results in blistering and bleeding of the feet.[74]

I should point out that most religions explicitly have an edict to not harm yourself, including Islam, Jainism, and Judaism. But each religion has practices that teeter on the edge and can give cover to the people in certain communities who choose to embrace the pain. The edict to not practice self-harm is also emphasized more today than centuries ago when pain practices were more prevalent.

Of course, most of these practices are substantially controversial, but the fact that they exist in many if not most religions suggests that there is a spiritual component to pain. While there are different reasons people give for these practices, several of them have been described as an act done to feel a connection to the Divine. Some Catholic saints, including Catherine of Siena and Julian of Norwich, teach that suffering can lead to spiritual enlightenment.[75] Religions such as Jainism and Hinduism have taught that voluntary acceptance of suffering as part of the act of penance ("tapas") is one way to achieve enlightenment, spiritual liberation, or even the attainment of supernatural powers ("siddhis") such as the ability to fly, shape-

---

72. Egan, "Being with Others," 15.

73. Gatrad and Sheikh, "Hajj," 136.

74. Glucklich, *Sacred Pain*, 37–38.

75. Glucklich, *Sacred Pain*, 29–30.

shift, or heal by touch.[76] People on the Sabarimala pilgrimage mentioned earlier have described a moment at which the pain disappears. It is replaced by overwhelming love and a union with the deity of the pilgrimage, Ayyappan.[77] Interestingly, a related phenomenon is reported in practitioners of BDSM, who have described religious ecstasy during moments of intense sexual pain.[78]

You can see from this that pain is a more-or-less universal way to connect to the Divine or the divine part of yourself. This is highly significant for magick, especially for those of us who believe magick comes from tapping into the Divine or our divine nature. It is also highly significant as a legitimate path for spiritual enlightenment. Most of the discussion about spiritual pain is done in academic publications, but I do definitely recommend the books below.

Some Further Reading

Sacred Pain: Hurting the Body for the Sake of the Soul by Ariel Glucklich. It is a phenomenal work, even if I don't agree with some of his views of spirituality.

Radical Ecstasy by Janet Hardy and Dossie Easton. This book is specifically on BDSM and religious experiences. *Warning:* Highly graphic portrayals of sex involving pain, including domination and submission.

The Significance of Pain for You

Okay, so I know some of you are thinking, "So what? That's never going to be me. I'm never going to stick hooks in my back." And that's

76. Bevilacqua, "Embodying Sacred Pain," 804; Wiley, "Supernatural Powers and Their Attainment in Jainism," 146.

77. Glucklich, *Sacred Pain*, 38.

78. Easton and Hardy, *Radical Ecstasy*, 9–10.

completely fine! Even if you are not interested in this kind of spiritual practice, I hope what I have just said has shown you that pain isn't necessarily a bad thing. In fact, it is something you can lean into, to great effect. So, don't let pain stop you, and use it for your magick!

If you are intrigued and want to explore pain as a spiritual pathway, I recommend reading the entire way through this chapter. There is a section at the end on exploring pain spiritually and incorporating it into your spellwork outside of tattooing. But since this is a book on tattoo magick, we'll explore energy raising specifically in the context of tattooing first.

Raising Energy During Tattooing

There are several ways to raise and send power during tattooing, using pain. You can surrender to the pain, or you can more actively engage with it. The former is the method that would lead to spiritual experiences, but these experiences are rare, and relaxing into the pain can be very counterintuitive for people. Even without the spiritual experience, though, it is quite powerful. I can attest to that.

I absolutely advocate practicing some of the exercises toward the end of the chapter. The pain of tattooing might catch you off guard. If you are getting a small tattoo, in the right spot, it might be over before you get into the groove!

If you try raising energy by surrendering to the pain, don't be disappointed if you don't have a profound experience. I did say it would be the way you'd most likely have a spiritual experience, but that isn't guaranteed. You can pursue that outside tattooing with the exercises at the end of the chapter, if you want. That or you can pay for dozens of hours of tattooing per month. I'm sure your artist won't mind.

Energy-Raising Technique #1: Muscle Tensing

Tensing muscles is a natural response to pain. Even if the tattoo is in an area that's not particularly sensitive, you're going to feel a twitch. If you're getting tattooed somewhere like the ribs or the elbow, you'll definitely be tensing up throughout your body. So use that.

I should say that tensing *on the spot you're being tattooed* is a bad idea. It will lead to more pain and may shift your skin, causing the needle to go somewhere it shouldn't. But say when you get your shoulder tattooed you feel tension in your arm. Lean into that more. Let your arm tense some more. You feel a twinge going down to your stomach? Contract your abs and hold your breath. See the tattoo pain as a magickal lightning bolt, tensing everything it touches, priming it for magickal release, activating your spiritual self. Once the artist has lifted the needle, relax and send the energy you raised.

Energy-Raising Technique #2: The Fire

Tattoo pain can feel like a burn, so use that visualization. The pain is a sacred spark, lighting the creative fire in you. Imagine the burn from the tattooing spreading throughout your body, lighting it up in brilliant red, orange, and white flickering light. Your body tingles with the transforming, sacred fire within. And when the needle is lifted, you visualize sending that transformative energy toward your outcome in a blaze of light.

Energy-Raising Technique #3: Lean Into the Pain

This is the technique that is closest to what people do when they have a sacred experience. When the needle is in, you might flinch. Your natural instinct is to move away from the pain. What you need to do instead is move toward it. Accept the pain. Relax into it. Experience the pain fully. Let your focus be as much on the pain as possible. All the while, keep your mind on visualizing a very simple representation of your outcome.

The sensations during this energy-raising technique are unpredictable, variable, and sometimes hard to describe. This could hurt more than the other techniques because you're focusing on the pain. You might find instead that it hurts a little less while you're focusing. This could be because as part of accepting the pain you're relaxing more at the tattoo spot. What you might also find is a weird sensation, where one moment you're feeling pain and the next absolute peace. This isn't dissociation because you are still focusing on the pain. It's what I call the beginning of a spiritual moment. For many of us, myself included, the peace will vanish in a moment or two, then come back, mimicking the peaks and valleys of a roller coaster. Finally, your experience might go a step further, leading to feelings of peace, expansion, and connection with the Universe. That is the true spiritual experience. I haven't experienced this yet, but I am working on it, and I hope you do too!

Whether or not you get to the spiritual experience, you are showing your dedication to your magick and your spirituality by even attempting it during the tattoo. You should be proud of yourself. And I can say from experience that the energy raised is quite profound.

Like I said in the last chapter, leaning into the pain is more effective as a means of raising energy when you have a particularly painful tattoo, like the one I got on my ribs. That's a pain you can't escape—one that can take up your entire mind, that you can lose yourself in more. This might not be a thing you want to hear. Attempting this experience might sound scarier now. But I'm saying it so you don't set yourself up for disappointment.

I cannot stress enough that you should NOT push yourself past your physical limits with pain and Witchcraft. There may be a moment when you find you can't focus on the visualization anymore. It's too draining. In that case, you can stop. You've done enough for the spell. Ask your tattoo artist for a break, and finish the rest of the tattoo focusing on the present or talking to your tattoo artist.

Practicing with Pain OR Exploring Pain Further as a Spiritual Practice

If you haven't gotten a tattoo before, the pain may take you by surprise. I don't recommend that you go into the appointment thinking, "I read how to do this; everything will go swimmingly." Instead, what I highly recommend is that you do a little bit of practicing with pain. That may sound very sinister, but trust me, it is very manageable. You also don't have to practice much, just enough for you to feel you've gotten the hang of it. You've got this.

There is, truth be told, a double motive to these exercises. What I am hoping is that some of you have been intrigued by the examples I gave at the beginning of this chapter about pain being spiritual. For one reason or another, you decided you want to explore the concept of pain more in your spiritual practice. You can do that through the exercises and tips below. There's even a spell and a meditation that incorporate pain.

The Key to Experiencing the Spiritual Power of Pain

I will reiterate something I said before: The key to experiencing the spiritual power of pain is the acceptance of the pain. To accomplish that, you have to do what you can to relax into it. You can't shrink away from the pain you experience; you must lean into it. One of the simplest things that helps is to change your breathing patterns. Exhaling helps activate a part of the nervous system that makes you calmer. You'll be able to better manage the pain if you do that. So, exhale during the pain. Your exhale should also be longer than your inhale to activate that part of your nervous system more.

When it comes to calming meditations that focus on breathwork, many people recommend a four-second inhale and a six- or eight-second exhale. That's a great place to start. Search "metronome" on your preferred search engine and select one of the links. You will see the option to set a BPM, or number of beats per minute. Set it to sixty and press play. Each click you hear is one second. Try inhaling for four clicks and exhaling for six. Do it a few times. It may be difficult at first, but trust me, you'll get the hang of it. When you feel you're starting to get it—and it may take a few sessions—set a timer for three minutes. When you can do three minutes of this breathing comfortably, you can stop. That will be more than enough for the following exercise. It is very relaxing, though, so I recommend doing it for ten minutes as part of your daily practice. You won't be disappointed.

For tattooing specifically, you're going to want to decrease the amount of time you draw in breath. Your tattoo artist is probably not going to give you that much time or warning before sticking you. Also, if they put the tattooing needle in and you didn't realize they were going to, you're going to want to draw in breath quickly so you can start to relax in the exhale. Set up the metronome, and for three minutes, try decreasing the inhale to three seconds. Bring it down to two seconds when you're comfortable. When you've gotten down to a time that you just can't seem to relax in or prevent yourself from moving during the inhale, then you'll know that the previous level is the sweet spot. For me, the sweet spot is two seconds.

Keep an eye on how your body feels and what moves when you breathe. If you draw in breath too quickly or in an unusual way, you might tense up in weird places. This is not good, especially if it shifts the skin. Experiment with changing the way you breathe, and note the effects. For example, try breathing from your abdominal area more. You could try to breathe into the sides of your rib cage or your back. When I got my rib tattoo, I realized quickly I was shifting my stomach and ribs too much. Not knowing what to do, for a little while I held my breath. Breathing more into my chest eventually provided a solution. If I had figured that out ahead of time, I could have saved myself a lot of discomfort.

This is probably where you're going to do some experimentation, because we all breathe differently. Go online and you will see people say slow and deliberate breathing is the key, but that doesn't take into account a few different aspects of how you breathe, such as what parts of your body move with your breath. Again, you will need to experiment to make sure magickal breathing isn't going to mess up your tattoo, or figure out how you can adapt.

With the following exercises, you control when the pain is, so you don't have to worry about suddenly breathing in, and you can experiment with the pain more beforehand so you know how and where you want to be breathing when it happens. You still should exhale, though, and slowly.

Your Tool for Practicing OR Exploring Spiritual Pain

The scourge, or flogger, has a history in Witchcraft as a painful tool to raise power. It is easy enough to use: Hold the handle and flick at the spot you want to hit. Personally, I'm not a fan. The conventional flogger you find online is not enough to cause a lot of pain to focus on. The pain doesn't last long enough for you to lean in. There are also a lot of things you can do to accidentally change the pain level, such as missing! That can mess with the momentum you're building or ruin a planned energy peak. In my experience, the point of the scourge seems to be more that the swinging of it can be hypnotic. I find it to be an interesting way to raise energy for magick and potentially effective, but it's not the kind of pain that parallels tattooing or leads to very powerful sudden experiences. If I'm working with pain or practicing for my tattooing session, that is not the way I like to raise power.

What I suggest instead is to use clothespins. They're simple enough: Just attach to your skin and take off after a certain period of time. They're also easy to find. Any conventional hardware store has them. Plus, they're cheap. They should be less than five dollars for a pack of fifty. A functional advantage of clothespins over the scourge is your ability to better set the pain level. The intensity will be different depending on the part of the body and how long you keep the clothespins on. In experimenting, then, you can get a sense for how to consistently make the pain a specific intensity. The exact amount of pain one feels will be different from person to person, especially because we have different tolerances for pain. I suggest a fair amount of experimentation.

Try seeing how the pain differs by location first. While you do that, use a timer so the difference in pain is based on location and not the amount of time they're on. I recommend at least three minutes. Try putting one on your stomach. Then your forearm. Your bicep. The top of your chest. Near the nipples.[79] Your ribs. Your thighs. See how painful it is in each spot. How tolerable is it? What is the experience of the pain? There are different pain sensations while it's on and when you take it off. Focus on both. If one placement is way

79. Don't put wooden clothespins on your nipples. If you want that, get specialty equipment.

too painful, you can avoid the spot or consider training yourself. I personally just avoid.

When you find out what spots work for you, try varying the time. You'll find after a little while that the pain of keeping them on will go down. For me it's about three to five minutes. That doesn't mean the area is numb: The pain when you take them off will only increase the longer they're on. *I would not recommend keeping them on longer than fifteen minutes.* You should only cut off circulation to one spot for so long, and much longer than fifteen minutes is not very good. If you want to increase the pain further, you can add more clothespins.

Ultimately, if you are just doing this to practice raising energy, you don't need to get the pain all the way to eleven. Make it painful enough that when you take the clothespin(s) off and immediately rub the area it creates a sort of burning sensation that doesn't go away for several seconds. If you are getting a tattoo on your ribs, shins, elbows, or knees, though, you may want to increase the pain level to prepare yourself. That *will* be distracting. Start practicing your energy-raising visualizations when you start to feel the burn after taking them off.

You may be thinking, "But Jake, there are a lot of other ways of causing pain that people do, such as holding on to combs or scratching or snapping with rubber bands." I have deliberately avoided many other kinds of pain that are too close to methods of self-harm. I do not advocate self-harm here, and I'm not about to make you potentially bleed. Rubber bands are very unwieldy in my experience. If you hit the wrong place, such as your fingers, that can be very distracting. A lot of these other methods don't really produce the kind of pain that lasts long enough for you to hold your concentration on and raise energy with. If you have another way you would like to use, please go for it, but using clothespins is the method I am most comfortable with and confident in. As I said before, if you have a practice of harming yourself out of compulsion or managing emotional pain, I sincerely hope you reach out for help.

Where Pain Fits with Your Spell or Meditation

There is nothing saying you have to use pain for spiritual purposes only when you are getting tattooed. If the idea of incorporating pain into your spellwork or meditations sounds appealing to you, I highly recommend you try it! You can use clothespins, if you want. Of course, the difference is with the tips I gave you, you're more practicing feeling the pain and staying focused enough to raise energy. Getting used to the pain is the goal there, not utilizing the pain. So, how should you work with clothespins for spiritual pursuits?

You can focus on the pain while the clothespin(s) are on or when you take them off. For the spiritual experiences I talked about earlier, the pain taking them off is more important. Having them on is just a slow, numbing pain. It's harder to lose yourself in it. Taking them off—especially if you've had them on for a while and have multiple—is that in-your-face, lose-yourself-in-the-moment pain. The pain lasts only for several seconds, though honestly that should be enough for most things. If you want it to last a little longer, you can rub the spot where the clothespin was. You can also put on multiple clothespins and stagger taking them off.

The intensity of the pain from taking off clothespins is like the intensity of the feelings I get when the energy I'm raising in a spell has peaked and is being sent off, so keeping them on for a while and taking them off all at once right at the end of the ritual works naturally with my style of working spells. If you want to re-create Deborah Lipp's female-power-sending method of raising and sending energy, maybe you keep the clothespin on until it *just* starts to get numb. Then, take off clothespins to release and put them back on elsewhere. I haven't been able to get that to work, though. Raising energy, even Lipp's method, still has to have (smaller) peaks and valleys. If I try to do that with clothespins, the time between the peaks is so long, and the number of peaks I need is so high that I cannot keep the focus, nor the conscious experience of raising energy. But it might work for you. So, feel free to try both out!

In sum, the key moment in your painful meditation and magick is the moment you take the clothespins off. You can focus on the pain while they are on to get that sense of raising energy. You can focus on them being on to prepare for the moment. But the action has to occur at the point of release.

I'm going to round out this section of the chapter with a spell and a meditation you can use incorporating pain. They are written in a more general format. That way, you'll be able to fit any intention or meditation in there.

A Spell with Pain

Note: This spell assumes you keep the clothespins on past the point when the areas go numb. Keep that in mind when planning placement and number of clothespins, with an eye to how much pain you want to feel.

Ingredients

Clothespins
A chant for your intention

Spell

Before the spell, you can feel free to decorate or add to the clothespins in a way that corresponds with your intention. Draw a sigil on them. Paint them a specific color, though let them dry before using. Tie a very, very, very light herb or tchotchke corresponding to the intention to one of the ends. Anoint the clothespins with oil and let dry. For spiritual pursuits in general, I frequently go with jasmine or frankincense essential oils. For magick in general, jasmine or cypress. For more specific intentions, I suggest you consult the correspondences table on oils in chapter 3 or experiment with oils to see which ones work with which intentions for you. And as I've said several times, no cinnamon, citrus, or peppermint essential oils.

Once you have set up, space has been made sacred, deities and other entities invoked, put yourself in a comfortable position. Relax with a few minutes of deep breathing: four seconds in, six seconds out. One by one, add the clothespins, starting with your less sensitive areas, such as the stomach and thighs, and moving up toward the top of your chest.

After you have applied the clothespins, sit with them. While keeping relaxed, focus on the pain. Accept it. Welcome it. See it as a sign of how dedicated you are to your intention. With every throb, feel your dedication increase. When the pain starts to subside, begin your chant. Ideally it will rhyme and have a consistent meter to keep you in your altered state better, such as:

With this pain I'm kept from harm.
All enemies shall be disarmed.
Protection will come from this charm.

Start quiet, slightly slower than your normal speech, and repeat the chant over and over. As you repeat, start to speed up your words and make your voice louder. Feel the energy pulsate, arising from the points where the clothespins touch your skin. The pulsating begins to grow. When you have reached the peak, with your visualization in your mind, take the clothespins off. Focus on the pain, the visualization still in your mind. Feel the moment the pain peaks—now that the clothespins no longer hold it back—when the energy surges out into the ether, to your goal.

Meditation with Pain

This will be a contemplative meditation. You should choose a concept to meditate on that is associated with pain. The following are examples: the relief that follows difficulty, the temporariness of pain or hardship, the necessity of suffering, and the source of courage in the face of danger. This, unfortunately, isn't a meditation that's very fruitful to record because the amount of time it takes to take off the clothespins, the number of clothespins you put on, and so forth, will vary a lot, not just from person to person but from instance to instance. However, the meditation is simple enough that you can learn what you need to do just reading this over a few times. So, keep going over the meditation text and grab those clothespins when you're ready to proceed.

Ingredient

Clothespins

Meditation

Relax, using deep breaths with prolonged exhales. One by one, add the clothespins, starting with your less sensitive areas, such as the stomach and thighs, and moving up toward the top of your chest.

While keeping relaxed, focus on the pain from the clothespins. Be mindful. What sensations do you notice? How do they change as you focus on them? How do they change from moment to moment? From clothespin to clothespin? As you shift your body? Keep your focus, thinking of the pain. When the pain starts to fade, keep your attention for as long as your experience says you need to feel the level of pain you want upon release. Then grasp the clothespin(s), inhale and, with the concept you are meditating on firmly in your mind, take the clothespins off.

Sit with your pain. Rub it in. Keep your question or concept in your mind. As the pain fades, let your mind drift. For ten minutes, or however long you need, notice your thoughts as they move about. If they drift too far from the focus of your meditation, gently pull them back. Note any profound thoughts in your head, or record the session and say aloud any association or insight you want remembered. When finished, make notes of what you thought about. A few hours later, or the next day, come back. See what insights you can glean from the notes.

…

I hope you found the subject of this chapter enlightening. Pain is a wonderful vehicle for so much change, and what better place to utilize it than during your tattoo. Now that we have talked about it, we have finished discussing energy raising during your tattoo session spell and the mechanics of working magick in the studio. But magick, frequently, doesn't exist in a vacuum. There are various ritual steps that accompany it, such as cleansing and consecration. If nothing else than for habit, you might want to conduct those steps with your spell. In fact, if your tattoo will be a devotional tattoo or an ancestor tattoo, a ritual will take outsize importance. But a tattoo studio is not your house, or wherever you do rituals. There will be restrictions. So next, let's take a look at making a ritual for your tattoo session.

11
Making a Tattoo Session Ritual

I did go over a lot in the last two chapters about casting a spell in the tattoo studio. As you know, though, spells exist within a larger ritual. You have your grounding and centering; casting a circle or making sacred space; the invocation of spirits, elementals, guardians, ancestors, deities, and so on; the spellwork; and then the thanking/departure of the beings you summoned and bringing down the circle. This chapter will help guide you through that.

Rituals are not just for magick. If you are getting a devotional tattoo or an ancestor veneration tattoo, you may want to make a devotional rite. If you just want a ceremony for every tattoo you get, whether or not it will be used in magick, you could make a ritual for that, too. This chapter will go over the different pieces that go into rituals so you can put them together into whatever is most helpful for the moment. We'll end with some example rituals.

Some Quick Housekeeping: Be a Courteous Person

You can do whatever kind of magick you want in your space. The tattoo studio is not your space. You are also not the only client who will be occupying it. So, you should be aware of how you can conduct a ritual while still being very mindful of the other people there and the restrictions that are on you. The customer isn't always right, and if you get really obnoxious, tattoo studios have the right to kick you out mid-tattoo.

While I'm positive you made sure your artist is cool with you practicing magick during the session, you can't control what clients walk through the door and what may make them uncomfortable. You also don't know whether they will judge you for your magick if they know what's going on. It is significant that one of the biggest maxims in Witchcraft is To Be Silent after a spell, because the negative perceptions of others may counteract your energies.

Because of this, I would caution you not to bring in a sword or athame. Don't use iconography that may cause very negative reactions, even if the items are sacred to you. Finally, don't shout the lines in a ritual, like "Oh Mighty Baphomet, I pray to you, come and inhabit your unworthy vessel. Wield your great power through me as I create this sigil to wreak havoc on my bitch mother-in-law!" (Honestly, I would be cheering on anyone I heard say that. I mean really, who the hell likes mothers-in-law? But I'm not many people.)

Discretion will take you very far where this type of magick is concerned. If you aren't normally a very discreet person, this may be a fun challenge for you: How can you work ritual in a way that others won't know what you're doing? It may require you to flex some creative muscles, but the increased effort toward your goal will only make your spell that much more powerful.

You should also keep in mind some people may have sensitivities you don't know about. Plenty of people might be allergic to incense or have sensitivities to smells, like my partner and the artist who did my blackout sleeve. You should consider not bringing incense *unless the tattoo artists say it's absolutely fine*. Even if you can bring incense, don't bring something you know other people will hate to smell. That is especially true for loose incense: There are very few things you can put on a charcoal brick that won't immediately smell awful. If you aren't aware of what the smell will be from an herbal blend, don't bring it. As a teenager, I used loose incense for years and thought it all smelled equally horrible. I did a ritual to Hecate where I burned dandelion and garlic and discovered *boy was I wrong*. The entire house smelled for three hours.

Please also be mindful of the tools you use. I know you're used to certain items being present for magick. Tattoo studios can be quite cozy, and there can be a lot of people moving around. You don't want anything to make it more cramped. You also don't want anything placed somewhere someone needs something else. And you definitely don't want to risk a fire, since your studio may have the wall covered in flash tattoo designs.

You should have a conversation with your tattoo artist about what tools you can bring with you. Include a discussion about where your things might be placed so you know ahead of time you won't be in someone's way. But before the discussion, take inventory and reduce the number of items you ask about to the *bare minimum possible*. You don't want to be pushy, and you don't want to pressure your tattoo artist into something just to please a client. Maybe you bring in a picture of any deity or being you want to invite into the space, rather than a huge statue. Maybe you have some pretty-looking crystal chips for each of the elements in your pocket and a small vial of blessed water for cleansing and consecration. There might be an item I didn't mention that is very important to you. But I wouldn't push for much more than this. And truth be told, all of these things together might be too much, especially for a small space. Clear anything with your tattoo artist. And know you don't need any tools to work magick, just your mind.

Finally, if your tattoo artist is a Witch, there is a chance they don't want you working magick during the session. Sometimes Witchy tattoo artists have their own magickal practices during tattooing, and your spellwork *as you present it to them* might interfere. If you feel strongly, you can find another tattoo artist. We don't want to pressure anyone to do something they don't want. But this also might be an opportunity to talk and find a fun, creative compromise.

Cleansing and Consecration

Any item used in magick works better if you have cleansed and consecrated it. Any cleansing and consecration is better as close to the spell as possible, so relying on the shower you took that morning might not cut it. But can you cleanse and consecrate your skin in the tattoo session? Absolutely! However, there are things you should be mindful of.

Let's start with cleansing. Cleansing will be slightly easier than consecration. Your tattoo artist will use soap on the area immediately before and during the tattooing. So, if you want to ask whether you can help clean, and visualize white light over the area you're cleaning, go for it! But you may get some confusion, because people don't tend to do that. You might also get resistance. You can always visualize yourself while they're doing the cleaning.

For consecrating, how about applying an oil or rubbing blessed water over the area? You know, the usual methods? Keep in mind that the tattooing machine will be making repeated small cuts. Bleeding is going to happen. Are you absolutely sure that what you are putting on the area is something you want going inside your body? Are you certain it's sterile? I'll answer that for you: It's not, so don't apply any to the area. That being said, you can consecrate yourself more broadly by applying oil or blessed water to your forehead, wrists, and heart. But you really should make sure your tattoo artist is fine with it.

What about cleansing the area with smoke? That is definitely an option if your tattoo artist is fine with it. Keep in mind there will be other people in the space, some of whom could be very sensitive to scents. If your tattoo artist is still fine with it, how you smoke cleanse depends on what part of the body is getting tattooed. If arms, legs, feet, and so on, hold the area above the stick so it catches the smoke directly. If it's a different part of the body, try holding the stick in front of you, letting the smoke permeate the area, then quickly and confidently walking through the smoke. That way, the smoke is getting on or near the area.

I personally do not use sticks for smoke cleansing, oils, or blessed water. I don't ask to use the soap. What I do instead is cleanse and consecrate by visualization and directing energy, rather than using any physical means. It's less likely to disrupt the tattoo setup. It's very subtle, and no one needs to know what you're doing, so you won't be making yourself feel self-conscious in front of other people in the studio. Finally, you're not putting anything on the tattoo that could compromise the sterility and mess up the tattoo. This method is what I very much recommend for all of you. If you feel strongly otherwise, though, feel free to go with what your heart says.

If you want to cleanse and consecrate energetically, find a color that you associate with the sacred. While the artist is setting up, focus on the area to be tattooed. Breathe deeply. Every time you inhale, I want you to imagine a white, cleansing gas going in your nose, down your throat, and directly to the patch of skin to be tattooed. Every inhale, you direct more cleansing energy down to the area. The white, gaseous energy accumulates so that shortly that body part itself begins to glow. Any energetic impurities or bad vibes that you see, feel, or sense are dissolved in the white light. Once you feel the cleansing is complete, say the following words. As you do, imagine the white light turning into your sacred color:

Blessed energy,
May this body be
Made sacred for this tattoo.
Blessed energy,
May this body be
Made sacred for this magick.
Blessed energy,
May this body be
Made sacred for my destiny.

By the time you finish speaking, the light has finished changing and the area is awash in colored sacred energies, infused in every pore and molecule.

Grounding and Centering

There are two methods for grounding and centering I'll give: the traditional method and my method. The traditional method is popular partially because it's so effective. In fact, it's so effective I made a variation of it in chapter 2 for you all to consciously charge your tattoos. But it's not the only way. In fact, it isn't what I use. It has been difficult for me to connect to those images personally because until recently I was used to living in a city, many floors in the air. The idea of extending my energetic roots down one hundred feet to concrete didn't feel like something I could anchor to. For an exercise where "ground" is part of the name, it just didn't work.

I'm going to give you an alternative, then: drawing in energy from the air. This is my method. Air is just as much a part of the earth as the ground is, contained within our atmosphere. All humans, most plants, and many animals utilize the air for many vital bodily functions. What I just breathed in almost certainly came from a tree a little while ago, which could have come from a field mouse, which came from a blade of grass, which came from a worm in little air pockets in the earth, which came from a flower, which came from another human ... on and on. The air we breathe connects us all in the same way the physical ground unites us. And it's available to us whether we're ground level, thirty-five thousand feet in the sky, or breathing old air in a submarine.

If it makes you more comfortable, you can record either of these meditations yourself. Just be sure to give yourself enough time while recording to sit with the sensations of each step before you move on to the next one.

Grounding and Centering: The Traditional Method

Sit down. Get situated. Close your eyes. Breathe deeply.

Imagine you are a tree. Feel your roots grow out of your spine, reaching downward until they hit the earth. When they reach the ground, the roots spread out. With every breath you take, they grow farther, in all directions. The more they grow, the more you feel connected to Nature. After a minute, take a deep breath in, visualizing energies from the earth rising through the roots and filling you. With every breath, you draw in more and more energy. When you have built up about as much energy as you can, send it up as new branches reaching up, up into the heavens. Keep growing the branches until you feel they have reached as far as they can. You are now the World Tree, the axis that connects all of creation, the center of the Universe. Feel yourself stretching throughout space and time. No matter where in the Universe you are, you are its center. Feel the Universe spinning around you.

When you are ready, on an exhale, bring your branches back down. Take the excess energy and on an exhale send it all into the ground. Retract your roots. They get shorter and shrink until they become a small ball that disappears up your spine. You turn back into yourself.

Open your eyes.

Grounding and Centering: My Method

Get situated. Close your eyes. Breathe deeply.

Focus on the tip of your nose. Breathe in deeply through your nose, then exhale through your nose. All the while, focus on the tip. Do you feel the slight tingling while you inhale? That's the living energy of the earth entering you.[80] The heat you feel as you exhale is all the negativity leaving your body.[81]

Breathe in again … and out. The tingling is the energy of all life that has touched this air—the trillions of organisms that touched the same particles of nitrogen, oxygen, and carbon dioxide. Through this air, through this tingling, you are connected to everything that is. Now that you are concentrating, knowledgeable of the energy in the air, you can direct your body to take in the energy. As the air settles in your lungs, the energy of life gets pulled into your body; this energy pushes any negativity there into your lungs, where it is exhaled out of your body. Silently, say,

Thank you for this air. Thank you for being a part of me.

Breathe in again … and out. Focus on the tingling. Focus on the heat of negativity escaping your body. Gradually, you will become more filled with the energy of life. At a certain point, you become full enough of life energy that the tingling even appears in your chest

---

80. Actually, it's the feeling of moving air across mechanoreceptors, but it works for our purposes.

81. It's body heat. But, again, a good metaphor!

and begins to spread throughout your body. Your arms tingle as you breathe ... your stomach tingles ... your legs tingle ... your face tingles ... the tip of your nose tingles. Your entire body is tingling with the energy of life itself, with the energy of trillions of organisms through countless eons. Take in one final deep breath, and let the energy out of your body as slowly as you can while focusing on the tip of your nose.

Sacred Space/The Magick Circle

Every year, it seems I see fewer people cast a circle for magick. That might be for the best in a tattoo studio. Even if your tattoo artist is usually going to be sitting in a chair next to you, there is nothing to say they can't move around. And they're often not the only ones in a tattoo studio. Other tattoo artists will be milling about, as will clients. You can't expect them all to respect the bounds of the circle—or even know it's there. And if you have to announce it to everyone who walks by, well, that's distracting and tiresome. What you can do, though, is make sacred space.

Since you almost certainly won't be bringing candles or incense, you can't be extremely formal about making sacred space. You also aren't going to be throwing salt everywhere; that's very messy for a high traffic, sterile area. So, you have two options I'll go over: You can ask some beings to establish sacred space for you, or you can direct your own energy. Just as you would use incense and blessed water to establish sacred space in the name of earth, air, fire, and water, so, too, could you ask the elements themselves, or elementals, to make the space sacred. Which option you want to go with is entirely up to you. I have done both to great effect.

Making Sacred Space: Method One

When you ground and center, in the part where you would release the energy to your roots or send it out in a final breath, do this instead:

Breathe in, and with a forceful exhale, imagine all the energy built inside you bursting out from you like a bomb of positivity, saturating the space you are in with positive energies. Make the sign of the equal-armed cross to seal them in. When it comes time to leave, see the energies throughout the space and make a prolonged exhale. As you breathe out, see the energies fade until they are gone.

Making Sacred Space: Method Two

Finish the grounding and centering as originally written. When the time comes in your ritual, lower your eyelids and say the following softly. As you chant, visualize the area being filled with white light:

On this very hallowed day,
Space sacred I shall make
A nexus for the energies
This Witch's rite will take.
I call upon the elements
Of east, south, west, and north
To walk around these sacred grounds
And bring this sacred temple forth.
Around, around, now go around
Space sacred I have cast
To take us to the Worlds Between
And unite the present with the future
And the past.
So mote it be.

When it comes time for you to leave, lovingly dismiss the elements.

Elements of the east, south, west, and north,
Thank you for joining me to make sacred space.
If you must leave me, please go with my greatest thanks and love.
Go if you must. Stay if you'd like. Hail and farewell!

You don't have to take down the sacred space, but if you or someone else wants you to, say the following. Visualize the light of sacred energies dissipating as you speak:

This day is done, as is my rite
Both to the greatest end
And so, to go back to the void
Space sacred I will send.
So mote it be.

Summoning and Dismissing Beings

There isn't too much to say for this section. Frequently when we summon elements, guardians of the watchtowers, elementals, the fey, ancestors, deities, and so on, we use a combination of words and visualization. These are both things you can do in a tattoo studio. You probably shouldn't be so loud about it, though, to be courteous of other people. It's probable you can't make huge, grand gestures, such as forming summoning pentacles. But if you mutter the words under your breath and visualize the gestures, you can go nuts. Remember: You are the magick. You can do all of this effectively in your mind.

Please, please, please, if you summon a spiritual being, do not forget to thank and dismiss them. Unless your tattoo artist is a Witch, they're not going to know how to do it if you forget.

Making Offerings

Offerings are standard in almost any ritual. Even in spells, you usually offer a little something to the spirits during cakes and ale. You might have an offering bowl at home into which you drop some of what you are drinking and eating. That probably works at home, but not in a tattoo studio. You are possibly going to be there for hours. Don't leave out a bowl in which bits of a sandwich are dissolving in juice over all that time. That's nasty to look at. Does this mean you can't make offerings? Of course it doesn't. But you probably should be a little stealthier. If you want to be the stealthiest, especially if your tattoo studio has strict food policies, offer up some loving energy to the beings who are there with you:

Bring up one of the happiest moments in your life. Go over the memory. Really try to lose yourself in the moment as if you are living it all over again. Feel the happiness bubble up in you. Move to another of your happiest memories, living that all over again. Then another. Then another, all the while feeling your happiness build. When you feel like your happiness can't build any more, visualize the beings you summoned for this rite in your mind's eye. Breathe in deeply, then exhale, letting all the happiness out. Visualize it being slung straight at them and that they absorb all this happiness you lovingly sent their way. Very softly, say, "Thank you."

If you don't vibe with that, the other option is to bring some food for after your spell is done and set aside a little bit of what you ate. Just pretend you couldn't eat all of it and box it up. When you get home, stealthily pour it onto the earth—or down the drain if you're in a city—saying softly, "Thank you." If you do this, check with your tattoo artist that you can bring food. I cannot guarantee they all allow this, though it's quite likely.

Setting Up a Devotional or Ancestor Altar

A lot of devotional and ancestral rites occur at an altar. This workspace and monument to love, awe, and reverence can contain a multitude of objects: representations, offerings, reminders of fantastic memories. You may remember I said there is very little space for much of anything at a tattoo studio. This is true. You also want to avoid things that draw too much attention because negative thoughts can undo magick. So, it would seem like having an altar at your tattoo session isn't doable. But what if I told you that you could have your altar with you and no one would know? Deities, ancestors, and other beings have a lot of associations that don't have to come in herb or candle form. In fact, some of them can be everyday objects, things no one would suspect are tied to Witchcraft. If there is a free ledge nearby, you can use it to build a stealthy mini altar.

Ancestors are the lowest hanging fruit for altar objects. No one would bat an eye at you bringing a picture of an ancestor to look at when you're getting a tattoo to remember them. Most people would actually find that really sweet. That there is your altar representation. Do they have a ring they passed down as an heirloom or something else small? Put that in front of the picture. Did they like turtles or seagulls? Get a keychain with one, attach it to your keys, and put it down, pretending you are just taking them out of your pocket to get more comfortable. Did they have a favorite color? If it's winter, bring a scarf in that color. Put it on the ledge, then put the ring and keys on top like you are just putting away some things to get situated. Place the picture there saying you wanted to look at it during the tattoo.

Deities wouldn't be very different, aside from the fact that bringing in a painting or photo would not be subtle in the slightest. The keychain idea I mentioned? That works for an animal sacred to that deity or if they have an animal form. A ring or some other jewelry works if it has a metal or crystal that is associated with them. If you are the kind to wear jewelry, wear enough rings to correspond to one of their sacred numbers if they have any. Do they have a sacred place? Bring a guidebook for "reading" in the waiting room, then lay that down where the scarf would have been. Without anyone being the wiser, you have created your own mini altar.

Example Rituals

Below are two example rituals that combine the advice I gave in this chapter. There is one example for spellwork and one for devotion. Feel free to use these as inspiration for your own thing or change a couple words to suit your needs. The first ritual is a lot stealthier than the second. There are even times where it's likely the tattoo artist wouldn't know what's going on. But I will repeat what I have said often: You need to tell them that you plan to work magick. You do. But just because they know doesn't mean you have to announce to the world what you're doing.

Example Ritual #1: A Ritual to Increase Psychic Abilities

You arrive at the tattoo studio on time. You want to set a good example and set the energies on the right foot, after all. Your tattoo artist comes out and shows you the design you originally agreed upon: an eye in a triangle surrounded by three full moons. They ask whether this is still good for you. You say yes. When they say they will be setting up, you ask how long they think it will take. Ten minutes, they say. Perfect. You ask them for a two-minute heads-up so you can go to the bathroom before they start. Of course, they say. Perfect. While they set up, you ground and center by focusing on the air flowing over the tip of your nose. In … and out. In … and out. Drawing in more energy. Always focused on the tip of your nose but feeling the tingling throughout your body.

The tattoo artist comes out to say it'll be two minutes. You walk back with them to their station, supposedly to put your stuff down before taking a bio break. The moment you reach the station, you send the energy from your grounding and centering out to the corners of the room with one final exhale. You take off your purple scarf, your silver ring, and a moonstone bracelet. The jewelry goes on top of the scarf and on top of your bag, which is on a nearby chair. Quick trip over to the bathroom, and you head back. You confirm the approximate time the tattoo artist thinks it will take. An hour, they reply. Okay, so you don't mind if I stretch? You rock to one side, then to the other. Touch your toes. Back up. You bring your arms into an X pattern on your chest and bow your head as if stretching inward. While in that pose, in three seconds, you mutter as softly as you can,

Lord of Magick, Great God Heka,
I ask you to be here today and give your blessing
to my tattoo for increasing my psychic powers.

You then push your arms skyward, your head looking up, bend over backward a bit in a supposed stretch, and mutter very softly,

Great Goddess of the Moon, Selene,
I ask you to be here today and give your blessing
to my tattoo for increasing my psychic powers.

Onto the tattoo chair you go. As they start to tattoo you, you feel the hum of the tattoo needle. Where once things were still, now the skin around the tattoo is vibrating. Slowly, the vibration spreads over more of your body. The vibrations in your body are rising, just as you are raising your vibration to better unlock your extrasensory potential. While this is happening, you visualize a silhouetted version of you, just a black outline. The only thing visible is your third eye, which is blazing in purple light. The energy centers in your body are opening. Your entire body is on fire with glorious sacred energy. The chakra in your visualization is becoming almost blindingly bright, and you feel a part of you unlock…

With the sending of that energy, the spell is done. You claim to the tattoo artist that you must be in a bit of a funny position because your muscles are cramping again. Could you quickly stretch for a couple minutes? Of course, they say. Back, forward, side to side. Down, up, and you reach to the sky, your head going upward back to the goddess position. As softly as possible, you say,

> *Great Goddess of the Moon, Selene, I thank you most profoundly for joining and helping me reach my full psychic potential. Go if you must, and always go with my love. Hail and farewell!*

And back inward, your head down, your arms in an X across your chest.

> *Lord of Magick, Great God Heka, I thank you most profoundly for joining and helping me reach my full psychic potential. Go if you must, and always go with my love. Hail and farewell!*

And out, your arms as wide as possible. You whisper,

> *May this sacred space bless whoever comes in it, if they wish to be, until its energies naturally dissipate. So mote it be.*

You get back onto the chair and let the artist finish up. They bandage you. You immediately head to the restaurant next door, and order some food. You set aside a portion for Heka and Selene, asking to have it boxed. When you get home, you set it outside as their offering.

Example Ritual #2: A Ritual to Honor Dionysus

When you searched for a tattoo artist, you specifically were looking for one who is openly Witchy. Luckily, there is an artist who is known in the local magickal community. You talk to them about the tattoo you want, how it will be to honor your chosen god Dionysus. They are very excited. They assure you that you don't have to be worried about privacy because they work in a private room. There is not much space, though. You also can't bring incense because it could get in the ducts between the rooms. That is perfectly fine with you. They give you a rundown of their usual magickal process for each tattoo, and you both determine your rite and theirs won't interfere.

You are there with them while they set up. Together, you two ground and center. As the studio is on the ground floor, they walk you through the traditional grounding and centering scenario, except this time, rather than a tree, you are a grapevine soaking up the energy of the earth. Without access to incense, to create sacred space and call upon the elements, you chant,

On this very hallowed day,
Space sacred I shall make,
A nexus for the energies
This Witch's rite will take.
I call upon the elements
Of east, south, west, and north
To walk around these sacred grounds
And bring this sacred temple forth.
Around, around, now go around
Space sacred I have cast
To take us to the Worlds Between
And unite the present with the future,

And the past.
So mote it be.

You pick a small vial out of your pocket. Grapeseed oil. You anoint your forehead and wrists, saying,

With these grapes, I make myself a worthy subject of my god Dionysus. May he tend to me like he tends to the grapes that make his wine.

You sit. As the artist begins to tattoo, you say,

Great Lord Dionysus, see this tattoo. Know that this is done in appreciation of you, in awe of you, in love of you. Bless us with your presence and bless this endeavor. So mote it be.

The fire of the tattoo begins to spread throughout. In a moment, you feel his presence move into you through the tattoo ink. This pain is divine fire. It's the heat of divine ecstasy. You revel in the pain, in initiatory energy, in enlightenment. Every moment you are grateful for the ability to share this experience with him. When the tattoo is done, you take out the bottle of wine and the figs you brought with you, as well as a plastic container. Your tattoo artist hands you a plastic cup. You drink half a glass to Dionysus's health and pour the rest in the plastic container.[82] You eat figs, leaving one in the plastic container in his honor. You ask your tattoo artist if they want you to keep the sacred space open. They say they don't need it, but you can leave it open if you like.

---

82. Clear this with your tattoo artist if you want to do something like this. Being drunk for your tattoo can cause complications such as increased blood loss and patchy tattoos, and drinking after tattoos can interfere with healing. Some tattoo artists are more sensitive to this than others. Mine is less sensitive. Yours might not be. A half glass won't get you drunk, but you should respect people's preferences.

Swiftly, you dismiss Dionysus.

Great Lord Dionysus. See this tattoo. See my love for you. Thank you for joining this space and joining with me. If you must leave me for now, please go with my greatest love. Go if you must, stay if you'd like. Hail and farewell!

One by one, you dismiss the elements:

Element of the [direction], *elementals of* [element], *I thank you for joining and helping me establish sacred space. If you must leave me for now, please go with my love. Go if you must, stay if you'd like. Hail and farewell!*

You leave the sacred space open. When you get home, since you live in the city and not near anything green, you dump the wine and figs in the disposal with a silent, secret prayer to the god who has blessed you.

...

You've now been through the process of getting a tattoo, from designing it, to timing it, to the ritual or magick you work during the session. So, we're done. Or are we? Not all ends are happy. That includes tattoos and spells. With that in mind, this next chapter will talk about touching up a tattoo that has dulled, covering up a tattoo you do not like, or reversing a tattoo session spell that you no longer want.

12
Touch-Ups, Cover-Ups, and Reversals

Tattoos are meant to be permanent, but that doesn't mean we don't want them updated from time to time. As tattoos age, the ink spreads, and you lose fine details. Tattoos also fade over time, especially if you are out in the sun. Sometimes, the artist misses a spot because of the blood or ink clouding their vision, or there is a minor imperfection. Get a touch-up to revitalize the color, fix any patchiness, or cover up the fact that the artist accidentally went a little past the stencil with the black ink.

Sometimes you really regret the tattoo, or the changes needed to update it will be too great to keep it. Your partner and you broke up, and now you can't look at the tattoo you got together in Paris without wanting to cry. Or you woke up from that bender in New Orleans, and you don't know whether you were drunk or the tattoo artist was drunk or both, but now you have a tattoo on your chest with "call me" and a phone number written on it. In any and all of these situations, a cover-up tattoo is warranted.

Finally, sometimes it isn't the tattoo you regret. Sometimes it's the spell you regret. It might have had some negative unintended consequences. It could also be you realized the intention you originally infused into your tattoo during the session wasn't something you wanted after all. Don't worry. It happens to the best of us. In those cases, you may want to reverse the spell. I will go over each of these changes to your tattoo in turn.

Touch-Ups

The main reasons to get a touch-up are significant fading, blurred lines, or patchiness in the ink. Really, though, even if the tattoo hasn't faded a lot, even if it's merely dulled, it is your prerogative to see what you can do to make it look crisp and vibrant again. Not every tattoo is going to need a touch-up, though. Black, navy blue, and other dark inks are less likely to need a touch-up. Thick lines are less likely to need a touch-up. People with darker skin tones are less likely to need touch-ups because melanin helps protect the ink from sun exposure. People who take care of their skin, who moisturize and wear sunscreen, are less likely to need touch-ups. People who keep their hands, feet, elbows, and kneecaps free of tattoos are less likely to need touch-ups. But the way a tattoo wears can be unpredictable. So, no matter who you are, you may need to get a touch-up for your tattoo now and again.

Let's start with fading, which is often the primary culprit for a tattoo having lost its sheen. Certain colors fade faster than others. White fades fastest, followed by yellow. Any lighter color, such as orange, or pastels, will also go away more quickly. White, especially, will fade so much that after a few years, it will often just look like someone's normal skin tone a shade or two lighter. There are several possible reasons, one of which is white is very reactive to sunlight. Another is that white ink particles are very large, making it hard to really pack a lot of it into the skin. Fine lines are also more likely to fade because there isn't as much ink there. Imagine you have a one-inch-thick black line, and you take out a couple millimeters on either side. You won't be too likely to notice. Now take a black line as thin as a piece of paper and remove the same amount. It will be gone! Tattoos are also more prone to fading on parts of the body where there is a lot of friction and movement. That includes the hands, feet, elbows, and knees. This kind of fading can also make lines look less crisp.

A tattoo can look patchy if your tattoo artist put different amounts of ink in different places. It is supremely difficult to saturate a large area of skin with the exact same amount of ink. If there are imperfections, they will become more visible over time. The tattoo's aging process can also make it look patchy. This is predominantly because the patches of skin fade at different rates. Are you outside a lot in a T-shirt? Is part of your tattoo covered by your shirt? Your tattoo will likely look a little patchy or unevenly faded where your sleeves end. If you wear a messenger bag to work and the bag rubs against a specific part of your arm, that spot will fade faster. You are a lot more prone to patchiness with fine line work. There isn't as much ink there, so any amount of ink loss is going to be more noticeable.

Blurred lines happen primarily when the ink spreads, or "bleeds," under your skin. Ink doesn't just stay in one place. Like a water drop on the floor, the liquid will spread. Unlike water, though, ink can take years to spread. The effects of bleeding will differ based on how thick the lines are. When a thin line bleeds, because there was so little ink in such a tight spot, it might end up fading. Thick lines aren't as likely to fade because there is so much ink in there already that bleeding isn't going to dilute it as much. But they will still bleed. The ink will still spread out a bit. This means a very detailed tattoo is less likely to age well if you have a lot of thick lines of ink. There's a lot more ink in thick lines that can spread, and it doesn't have to spread far before it covers the space and you can't make out details of the design.

When it comes time to touch up your tattoo, there are several things your artist can do. If you have faded lines, making the line again will bring that sharpness back. If the lines have blurred or bled, you might need to thicken the line to cover it up, though that is a slippery slope. If the color is the problem and there is minimal fading, it's often as easy as a fresh coat of paint. One more layer of color, and presto! Rejuvenated, brightened, flawless. If the color has faded unevenly, that will be more difficult. People sometimes might not have the exact shade of ink, and a lot of light blue with a little dark blue can look rather different from a little light blue with a lot of dark blue. But a good tattoo artist will know their color theory well enough to appropriately rebalance the color. Sometimes it isn't fixing the color or the line work that will give a tattoo life again. Sometimes some new small details, such as adding in shading, will do the trick. In any case, you will be in good hands with a competent tattoo artist.

So, when do you get a touch-up? Some types of damage will happen faster than others. Going into a chlorine pool a week after getting your tattoo will cause a lot of fading—and so will tanning a week after your tattoo. If you do screw up right after getting the tattoo, be patient. I know you want to run to your tattoo artist immediately—and you should let them know now—but you're going to want to wait. You should not get any touch-ups until the skin has fully healed, which can take four to twelve weeks.

Be patient, too, if there's something wrong with the way the tattoo looks. Tattoos take a little time to settle in, so I've seen. When I got my blackout sleeve, I couldn't stop noticing what I thought were imperfections in the ink saturation. I would stare at it, frequently turning my arm to get a closer look though I'd seen it many times before. But my tattoo artist at the time seemed really pleased with it. So, I decided to wait, in case he knew something I didn't. A few months later, I couldn't tell that anything was ever wrong. Sometimes a little time is what it takes. Bottom line is: You can touch it up whenever you want as long as it's been at least four to twelve weeks. Don't do it more often than every ten years, though, if that. Your skin can only hold so much ink, and it will bleed more if you push it past that point.

So, what does this mean for the magick that is imbued in the tattoo? Should you be concerned that it won't be as strong if it starts to fade? Not necessarily. If the only magick you worked with the tattoo was in the tattooing session, that spell was one and done. You aren't doing any ongoing work with it, so it doesn't matter what it's turned into. If this is a tattoo you want to work with in the future, of course the ink is a part of it. A big piece, though, is the tattoo as a symbol. That symbol, and its connection to your subconscious, won't go away so easily, no matter how faded it is. If you want, though, you could hold a mini ritual during the touch-up session to re-imbue it with magickal energy. I have that down here.

Ritual to Re-Imbue a Tattoo with Energy During a Touch-Up

If you don't remember any of the visualizations you've used with this tattoo, come up with a new one. The only rule is that it must encapsulate the intention you typically work on with this tattoo. While the tattoo artist works on your tattoo, feel the sacred fire of the pain in your tattoo. Feel it kindle the energies within, the vibration and prickling pushing new life into the tattoo. Keep the visualization in your mind while you repeat the following:

What once was faded now once more
Infused with life, power galore.
New energy, in magick be
Open to me, so mote it be.

Cover-Ups

I'm not a professional tattoo artist, and I don't know the specifics of your tattoo, so I'm not about to give advice about what can get covered up and how. You should know cover-ups can be quite expensive. This is especially true if you need to get the original tattoo faded through laser removal first.

While you're getting the tattoo covered up, why not do some magick? The act of covering up goes really well with a banishing intention. It could also be good for a life change, since that's what's happening to your skin. If you want to do a banishing spell, you don't need to worry as much about the design of the tattoo that goes on top. It's what you're getting rid of that is the focus. That said, black is a good color for banishings, and cover-ups tend to need to be darker colors. So, a blackwork tattoo or even a blackout wouldn't be a bad idea for the new design. If you want to focus on a life change instead, the tattoo over top will be extremely important. You want to make sure it reflects the change you want to make as much as humanly possible. Take your time with the design. Think it through a lot.

If you are going to do a cover-up, I would be picky about who does it. Cover-ups are more difficult than a normal tattoo. Think about the knowledge it takes to know how different inks will look over differently shaded skin so you can mix up the right color for the final look. Now think about how different inks will look mixed with any other color, of any shade or saturation. Your new tattoo is *not* going on top of the other one, after all. It's all going to mix together. And that's just the coloring! You see how this can be a delicate business?

You should also keep in mind that even if you find a good artist, not all tattoo artists are willing to do cover-ups. This is partially because they are so difficult and so much can go wrong. Cover-ups also don't always look the best; they definitely don't look as good as a fresh tattoo does. And tattoo artists, especially the social media savvy ones, like to make sure all their work looks good. Yes, if it doesn't look good it's not their fault; it's because it's a cover-up. You know this. But someone else might not. If they ask who did your tattoo, are you going to say, "Who wants to know? You think it looks like crap?" before you respond?

This is all a long-winded way of saying: Find a specialist. And ask a lot of questions. And listen to their advice. If they say you should get laser removal to fade it first, look into laser removal. Sure, get a second opinion, but if the second person has a different opinion, you know what you need to do? Find a third person to be the tiebreaker. Don't assume your opinion is the tiebreaker. You don't know tattoos anywhere near as well as they do, and the person who said it will be fine might be dead wrong.

People don't always want to get a cover-up because they regret something about their tattoo. If you get a lot of tattoos, you will eventually start to run out of room. If you have a killer design you absolutely have to have, you might just cover up one of the old ones. There's nothing wrong with making space for the new.

Below are some rituals you might find useful if you are about to do a cover-up.

Ritual to Make Space for a New Tattoo or Retire a Tattoo You No Longer Want

On the day of your tattoo appointment, gather a wet wipe and, if you drink, a glass of champagne.[83] Stare at the area of skin that will be covered up. Make a toast to that tattoo. Tell yourself the story

83. As I said in the last chapter, drinking a lot before a tattoo can have negative repercussions. Some tattoo artists are more comfortable with it than others. Check with your artist beforehand.

of that tattoo and what got you to get it. Tell any good stories you have of that tattoo, such as the first time someone complimented it. When the champagne is almost gone, put it aside. Take the wet wipe and swirl it on the skin counterclockwise. You are wiping the area clean, a blank slate for your new tattoo. While you rub, say thank you one last time to your old tattoo. Put the wipe aside. Look into what's left of the champagne. Stare at the bubbles of carbon dioxide floating to the surface, like tiny exhales. Charge the champagne with the intention of breathing new life into that area. When it has been charged, pour the champagne on the skin.

Ritual to Banish a Bad Tattoo

When it comes time for the tattooing to start, stare at the old tattoo. Keep it in your mind. Make sure the image stays there. If there were any negative feelings attached to this tattoo, I want you to imagine them. If you can, that is; we're avoiding trauma. Feel the emotions more and more. Feel them as hard as you can. If you are angry, imagine your skin turning red. If you are sad, imagine blue. If you are embarrassed, yellow. When you think you've peaked, know that these feelings aren't part of you. They are part of the tattoo. See the visualization fall away from all parts of you except the patch of the skin that is being tattooed. The only part that is a different color is the tattoo.

In your head, begin to chant the following:

You weren't[84] *good,*
That I regret,
But things will really change.
Away you go,

---

84. Pronounced with two syllables—"were-ent."

No one will know
You ever were so strange.

As your artist goes over the area, see that any place they go over with their needle is no longer red or blue or whatever. The unwanted influences of that tattoo have fallen away, banished by your new tattoo. Your chanting will eventually fade. That's fine. When that happens, just sit with your happiness over the fact that you have banished that negative part of your life.

Making a Change with Your New Tattoo

This ritual is for times when you are both banishing an old tattoo and bringing something good with the new tattoo. You can't just concentrate on the banishing during the tattooing. It's not like they're covering something up and then once that's done they're going to make a third tattoo over top of it. By the time the banishing is done, the tattoo will be over. At the same time, you don't want any residual feelings from the old tattoo to mess up the feelings and energies that get into the new tattoo. You need a bridge between them.

I want you to imagine how having this new tattoo, or having the intention behind it come true, will make you feel. Take some time over a few days to really think about it. Try to conjure this feeling in you. This will be easier for some of you than others. What may help is to try to find a memory where you most strongly had that feeling. It should be strong enough that thinking of it makes it easy to invoke. Immerse yourself in that memory whenever you think "I want to feel [insert your feeling]." Practice bringing up this emotion. Unlike the other times in this book when we raised emotional energy, this kind of practicing beforehand is necessary because you need to conjure the feeling associated with your new tattoo very quickly.

When it comes time for the session, stare at the old tattoo. If there were any negative feelings attached to this tattoo, I want you to imagine them, starting approximately thirty seconds before your artist begins. Feel the emotions more and more. Feel them as hard as you can. When the artist starts to move the tattoo needle toward your skin, inhale. When they start tattooing, exhale and feel all of those negative sensations leaving with the breath. Then, bring up the new feeling *immediately*. Maintain that feeling as long as you can. When your artist goes to put more ink on the needle, inhale and let yourself come back to neutral. When they start tattooing again, exhale again and bring the new feeling back *immediately*. Repeat until you have no negative feelings while you look at the tattoo. When this happens, you've reset the emotions associated with the tattoo. You're clear to start raising energy for the new spell.

Reversals

We've all cast a spell that made us think, "Maybe I should change that ..." Maybe you hexed someone you thought was mean to your friend only to find out there's a slight possibility they were teasing (Like a friend did to my partner! Jay, it's still your fault you crashed). It could be you realized you used the wrong ingredients or were saying something you didn't mean to say. Maybe you accidentally formulated the spell in such a way that it might end up hindering you. For all of these, assuming the spell hasn't come to fruition already, you should simply reverse it. You are probably familiar with a few ways of undoing spells, such as taking the spell ingredients apart or lighting them on fire. Those methods probably won't be good for your own skin, though, so I have the following ritual. If you need to reverse a tattoo spell, don't be disappointed or beat yourself up. It may have been expensive. But it still looks sick.

Sometimes we have cast spells that were regrettable but weren't a big deal. We can simply undo them. No harm, no foul. Sometimes, we cast a spell that we know we really shouldn't have. Spells that target people's free will and baneful magick are the most frequent in that category, though many of us don't have a problem with a good curse when deserved. Many of us—if not all—have made a spell we feel very guilty about. Even if you reverse the spell, you should remember the tattoo is going to stay on your skin and be a reminder. If you can't take a look at it without feeling guilty or embarrassed, I would encourage you to talk to your therapist about it. If you can't do that, you might look into getting the tattoo covered up. Shit happens, and you shouldn't beat yourself up about it. Just be a little more careful next time!

Ritual to Reverse a Tattoo Spell

For this, all you will need is a black permanent marker and a black chime candle, plus something to light it. How thick of a marker depends on how big the tattoo is. Optionally, you can use some olive oil and rosemary—dried if infused in the oil, fresh or dried if you're just mixing it in the oil right before the spell—to dress the candle.

If you have the optional ingredients, take a pinch of the rosemary, and grind it down using a mortar and pestle. Transfer to a flat surface. Use the olive oil to dress the candle. For banishing and cleansings, I will usually apply the oil from the top to the bottom in one motion. Use whichever method works for you, though. Once the candle is dressed, roll it lightly in the herbs so they stick to the candle. Use a very small amount of rosemary; the more herbs you put on there, the bigger the fire hazard is. Empower the candle and the permanent marker for cleansing. Light the candle.

Look at the tattoo. Actually, look past it. Soften your gaze, like I talked about in chapter 2. Bring the intention to mind. Now, with your gaze softened, visualize those energies pulsing gently within the tattooed skin. See and feel those magickal energies swirling around. Pick up the black permanent marker. Uncap it. With one dramatic movement, draw a line through the tattoo. See that the energies stop where the line is. They have been absorbed by the marker. Make another mark. See that the energies aren't there anymore either. With another mark and another and another, gradually fill in the tattoo with black permanent marker. Make sure you use deliberate, dramatic strokes every time. No running it over the tattoo back and forth. When you are done, the feeling of the intention should be fully gone. Absorbed by the marker.

Cap the permanent marker. As you do, see with your mind's eye the energies the marker absorbed radiating from it. Pass it repeatedly over the candle's flame, about a foot above. As you do, see the heat burn away the energies it absorbed. Be quick about moving it over the flame and do not put it directly into the flame. One foot above—and capped, because permanent ink has a high alcohol content. Chant:

Once bound in ink
Destroyed in heat.

When the energy has peaked, or you think everything has been burned away, set the marker aside. When the candle finishes burning, toss the marker. When the top layer of skin above the tattoo flakes off, the tattoo will remain, but the spell will be gone.

Unfortunately, we have come to the end of what I have to tell you about tattoos. But before I leave you, I want to instill something in you: Permanent isn't the only way to use body decoration in magick. So, this next, final chapter will be about temporary forms of body decoration.

13
Magick with Temporary Body Decoration

I'm going to go out on a limb and say something that shouldn't be controversial: Permanent is not the only way to go for magick. Any sort of body decoration can be used as a spell. Tattoos are powerful magickally because they are potent symbols, and they have a greater connection to you as an actual part of you. Temporary body decoration doesn't have the same connection as tattoos, but they are still potent symbols in their own right.

Actually, temporary decoration has a special advantage in smaller, short-term magick. Tattoos are expensive and permanent. Getting one is a big commitment. Unless it's a versatile tattoo you can use later, you might be better served getting a tattoo for a bigger or long-term goal. There are times, though, when you want to work magick and the outcome is something small that you need in this moment. Once the event passes, you don't need the effect to persist. Let me give you an example: Right now there are three blue tea light candles burning on my left. I burn these candles whenever I write for good communication and overcoming blocks. In the bindrune tattoo on my wrist, I have also traced the Ansuz rune in blue for communication.

That's all I need right now. I don't have contracts for multiple extra books. I don't know whether or when there will be a second book, let alone a seventh. If I knew that, maybe I would get a tattoo for writing. But right now, I just need to worry about proper communication and writing while this document is open.

There are so many reasons you might be interested in this chapter. I'm letting you know they're all valid. Maybe you're not ready for a tattoo. You picked this up because you're dabbling in the idea, but you aren't fully there yet. No sweat. Tattoos are an investment. They're expensive. They're permanent. They're painful. If you don't feel ready just yet, waiting is a wise decision. Instead, use this chapter, and draw the design you're thinking of on yourself. Maybe instead you have a tattoo but aren't ready for your next one. Again, perfectly fine for the same reasons as before. Maybe it's not the tattoo. Maybe this book has gotten you interested in starting Witchcraft. You've read everything in this book and ordered other books. But with your magickal comfort level being what it is, doing something permanent seems really daunting. Totally get it. No matter what, you do what you're comfortable with. In the meantime, ease into it by using temporary decoration since it evokes a similar vibe. I might also recommend working pain magick, which I talk about in chapter 10. If you weren't a Witch, you likely came to this book as someone who likes tattoos, so you're used to the pain. The magick in chapter 10 might feel comforting in its own way—or even powerful!

There are many ways to decorate your body temporarily. Right now, I'm going to go over the ones most similar to tattooing. In addition to being good for shorter term magick, each form of decoration has its own area of expertise. Each method has its own associations, whether it's a characteristic of the material or where and how it's used. Since a lot of magick is symbolism, that means each of these might be more suitable than tattoos under specific circumstances.

Temporary Tattoos

How many times did you put on temporary tattoos as a kid? For me, it was all the time, which was kind of ironic, because my mom was adamantly against tattoos and later on would say she'd cut me off from college if I got one.[85] She was probably fine with those because they were—say it with me—temporary. It made them seem less consequential. But that doesn't mean your magick with them would be.

Temporary tattoos can be good practice for seeing how the tattoo will look on your skin. Sounds weird, right? The temporary tattoos you buy only come in so many designs, don't they? Luckily, there are websites that will make custom temporary tattoos for you. To my knowledge there isn't one where a tattoo artist will sit down with you and make up a design that you can turn into a temporary tattoo. But they do allow you to upload images, which gives you a lot more versatility. Maybe the (non-copyrighted!) images you find on the internet won't correspond exactly to what you want, but they will be close enough to experiment with. Some companies even have simple platforms that allow you to draw out your design.

Say you have something you are regularly doing over the short-term future, which requires the same kind of short-term spell. If you want, you can put together a sigil, upload it, and order a dozen or so temporary tattoos to have at your disposal whenever you need them. My writing session magick would be a good example. This method has the added benefit that the symbols will look the same every time; the same cannot be said for marker.

One of the particular advantages of temporary tattoos over any other body decoration in this chapter is they do a much better job at covering up what is already on the skin, since they lie on top of it. So, they can function well for any spell that involves "covering up" what's

85. Happily, she has mellowed and is now considering getting one of her own!

underneath. Are you about to do a glamour? Want to come across as someone new? Get a temporary tattoo that corresponds to the glamour you're trying to adopt. In the spell, note that the tattoo is your glamourized self covering up your current self for the duration of the spell. Another example: Is there a scar you're trying to lessen? Get a temporary tattoo that corresponds to healing, and cover the scar completely with it. You are "covering up" the scar you hate. When the tattoo washes off, the scar will be lessened, if not completely gone. Are you trying to banish something in your life and replace it with something more beneficial? Write something on your skin that represents what you're banishing and cover it up with the temporary tattoo. In that case, probably best to use a marker that is very weak so by the time the tattoo comes off, the marker will be gone.

One of the downsides of temporary tattoos is once you have landed on a design, you can't change it for a while. Say I realize the temporary tattoo would correspond to my intention a lot more in a different color? Or the text doesn't jive with me when I see it? I would have to make a new design, pay all over again, and wait for it to arrive. I wouldn't have that issue with marker. If you see yourself as more indecisive or more spontaneous, temporary tattoos might not be the right route for you.

If you're economical, you should pay attention to price. Even a very tiny one-by-one-inch temporary tattoo could run you five dollars. The larger you need it, the more expensive it will get. If your temporary tattoo is supposed to have text, depending on how much text there is, you would need a fairly big tattoo for it to be legible. This is especially the case if it's in a very flowery script. Yes, there are discounts for buying in bulk, but again, once you lock in, you're stuck with it until you run out or buy an entirely different design. If you are on a budget while saving up for a tattoo, this wouldn't be the medium I would suggest.

Henna

Henna is used throughout the world as a semipermanent dye. There are too many countries with cultures that use henna to list. Malaysia, Morocco, Armenia, Afghanistan, Turkey, the UAE, and India are just some examples. If you come from South or Southeast Asia, the Middle East, North Africa, or parts of Eastern Europe, you may come from a culture that utilizes henna.

All of the traditions for henna can be distilled into a few uses:

Marking celebrations: Applying henna to the skin for a bride occurs in regions as diverse as Afghanistan, Armenia, and Algeria. Skin is dyed with henna for holidays such as Diwali in India and Eid al-Fitr in the Middle East. While henna traditions for weddings frequently focus on the bride and women in general, the groom can be adorned too.

Decoration: In Pakistan and Morocco, henna isn't just used to decorate for weddings. It's something you'll find every day. In Morocco there are henna dealers who will dye tourists and make their living doing it!

Dye: Henna can dye hair a beautiful orange color. It will also dye fingernails, which has been done as far back as ancient Egypt. In Islam, using henna to dye one's beard once it has turned white is officially sanctioned and encouraged.

Magickal act: In Morocco, applying henna is believed to bring luck and joy. This is one reason it is applied to brides there. In Armenia it brings fertility. In the Sudan it is applied to ward off evil spirits.

Is henna cultural appropriation? This is a very thorny question. I will say henna is not specific to any one culture or even group of cultures. Henna is applied in dozens of countries across three continents, from Malaysia to Morocco, including to tourists. It is much more associated with one or two specific cultures, at least in my experience. That might be why some people may see it as cultural appropriation. But in actuality, it doesn't belong to one culture or even several. This is definitely one of those times to ask how equipped you are to handle someone confronting you about your henna being cultural appropriation.

It's at this point, in talking about what people believe should or should not be done, that I should point out the FDA has approved henna only as a hair dye. This is because many commercial henna mixtures can have additives that are not safe for the skin. Natural henna paste might be fine, though many commercial products will pretend to be all-natural to pass various regulations in other countries. This is all to say that you should be very careful. Never ever apply henna that's been colored, such as black henna. Do a lot of research to see if a henna applier you're thinking of uses all-natural henna, or do it yourself. Even if you do it yourself, do a lot of research on the henna you use. I cannot guarantee anything about the safety of the henna you use. And know that applying henna yourself isn't illegal. The FDA won't come after you if you do it only for yourself in the privacy of your home. They might confiscate a shipment of henna if they think it's used for something other than the hair, but that is rare.

If you were to apply henna to your skin, know that henna is much better than any other temporary decoration for life events, long-term goals, and rites of passage. You want to become a vice president in your field? Make a henna pattern for the goal and apply it to your body somewhere discreet for your yearly reviews. Apply it when you are learning skills that will increase your performance. Apply it before job interviews for a promotion, whether at your current company or an opportunity at another company. And every time you have succeeded at one step along your goal, go out and celebrate with the henna pattern on you. Acknowledge each rite of passage that is a new role, using your henna.

Magick Marker

The third option I will cover is to use marker. I'm guessing many of you have some colored pens or markers lying around. Most of you even have a black permanent marker. So, this medium is readily available to you. And hey, if you don't have those things, you can just go to a local store. Another great thing about magick marker is its price. If you don't care about getting the best markers that money can buy, a set will cost maybe twenty dollars. Markers can also be quite versatile in color. Most colors you could want should be readily available in a set of twenty-four or forty-eight, unlike henna, which is only red/orange/brown.

Magick marker has a crucial advantage not just over other temporary decorations but over actual tattoos. Tattoo inks, at least for now, do not come in fluorescent. They don't come sparkly or in metallic shades. They definitely don't glow in the dark. Part of the reason is the ingredients for those would be toxic if placed in your skin. Markers do not go under your skin, so they do not have those limitations. Technically, some temporary tattoos can come in these types of colors. They tend to be much more limited, though. Can't beat the versatility of marker!

When we talk about color magick, we often don't go over sparkle, fluorescent, or some metallics. So, here are their correspondences all in one place:

Metallic, Fluorescent, and Sparkle Correspondences

Color	*Correspondences*
Silver	Psychism, spirituality, the moon, cycles, balance, illusion
Gold	Success, prosperity, the sun
Copper	Love, creativity, fertility, Venus
Sparkles	Glamour, illusion, innovation, prosperity
Glow in the dark	Finding what is lost, protection, absorbing energy
Blacklight (UV)	Invisibility

Think through whether you want to use a temporary or permanent marker. Temporary marker is good for a day, maybe two. Permanent marker will stay on you until the skin it's on flakes off, which is a few weeks. Temporary marker might be better for a short-term goal. If you like to forget about your spells after you cast them, a temporary marker would be best. Temporary marker is also great for goals or intentions that keep changing. As I mentioned in chapter 7, I use temporary marker on the tattoo I have for daily affirmations. If you want to use permanent markers for magick, keep them away from lips, eyes, and other delicate areas. If you have sensitive skin, avoid them entirely. The chemicals in them are generally fine, but they can irritate sensitive skin.

You might remember, way back in chapter 2, I talked briefly about modifying the tattoo you already have with marker to shift the intention. And why not? If your tattoo functions as a visual symbol and you take a marker to it, that symbol has been changed. Take a tattoo that is an empty circle and color it in to correspond to a moon phase whose energies you want to channel. Put a giant black "X" over your heart tattoo for a cord cutting or a hex. Or draw a heart next to it for a love spell. Or draw a house around it for security and stability.

Remember the chapter I had on magickally versatile tattoos? How do you activate a given intention in your versatile tattoo? If you have a matrix tattoo, you're probably going to want to draw the intention in it, in marker. If the tattoo is a series of separate symbols for different intentions, you could get away with tracing the correct one with your fingernail. It is much more powerful, though, to highlight that part of the tattoo with marker. Think back to the cornucopia of herbs tattoo from chapter 7. Perhaps when you want to be calm, you pull out a light purple marker and color in the lavender flower. You concentrate on the feeling you want to evoke as you color mindfully. In this case, the thinner the marker, the better.

Makeup

Remember how I said you should avoid marker over sensitive parts of the skin such as the eyes and mouth? You know what does work on there? Makeup! You can find tips on makeup in books on fashion magick, such as *Glamstrology* by Michael Herkes. A full treatment is beyond the scope of this book. But since it is temporary body decoration, and it can be used in magick, I have a few things to keep in mind.

First, you can put the makeup where it typically goes, or you can use it the same way you use a marker. You might not have markers in your bag while out, but you more likely have some lipstick or eyeliner. Just draw a sigil or other representation of your outcome somewhere discreet. Alternatively, if you are applying it on your face like you typically do, and you have much better coordination than I do, feel free to draw a sigil with it, then cover it up when actually applying the makeup. Blend as needed to cover up the sigil extra well.

If you are going to apply to the skin, eyeliner is probably the easiest way to draw something.

Second, keep in mind that makeup can rub off on clothes. You know those social media ads where someone applies makeup to their arm and tries to rub it off to show it doesn't get on their finger? I wouldn't necessarily trust that over the course of many hours, at least not under your favorite shirt or pants. Setting spray may help, yes, but think about how you feel about that magickally. Is the setting spray just keeping the makeup from going onto your shirt, or is it a barrier trapping the magickal energy of the sigil? Whichever one you decide is the one that's right for you, but do think about it. Now that being said, there is nothing saying you have to apply it for going out. You can wear it skyclad in ritual as another tool to boost your intention—provided you work skyclad, of course. You can also wear it at home in a place you think you aren't likely to have it rub against something.

Third, for correspondences, you want to think about two things: what the color is and where it is typically applied. For color, you can refer to my correspondence tables in chapter 9 and this chapter. For correspondences for where it is applied, anything on the eyes might be for clarity, protection, psychism, and baneful magick, if you practice it. The mouth would be for communication, deception, authority, and success. The neck would be for stability, support, communication, leadership, and open-mindedness. The cheek would be for protection, as are the eyebrows.

Raising Energy with Temporary Body Decoration

When we talked about tattooing, we talked about raising energy through the pain or through the vibrations. We don't have those with temporary body decoration, so what do we do to raise energy?

Raising Energy with a Temporary Tattoo

After you've wetted the back of the temporary tattoo with a sponge, you have to press firmly on the area for at least thirty seconds. Start pressing mildly, with the visualization in your head. You can start a simple chant as you do it, such as:

Cell of paper, warm and wet,
Contains my goal, which I now set.
In just one sec, you shall be free,
And my desire shall come to me!

Keep repeating the chant to raise energy. When you feel the energies are the highest they can go, at the same moment stop chanting and take the paper backing off of your new temporary tattoo!

Raising Energy with a Marker

As you draw or color, stay in the moment with your intention firmly in your mind. At the same time, feel the marker move across your skin. Feel the slight tickle of the applicator. Every cell that is being passed over by the marker is pulsing with energy. It's the energy of the Universe, funneled through your concentration to give it form and function, to shape it and send it off into the world. As you are doing this, if you feel you can, start a simple chant like the following to raise energy, coupled with the sensation of the marker:

Every stroke and every color,
Brings me safely to another
State of mind and state of world.
My goal desir'd shall now unfurl.

You can stop the chanting when you have finished drawing or coloring. If you feel it is not time yet, put down the marker and keep chanting. When you feel the energies have reached their peak, send them off!

Raising Energy with Makeup

This will be almost identical to what you do with marker. You're just going to have to focus on the feeling of the applicator on your skin, which might not be as fine or focused as a marker. If you are applying over a larger surface area, such as when using foundation, I want you to visualize the makeup as the energies of the Universe being deposited on your skin. It tingles and pulses with channeled potential. As it sits, you feel the sensations begin to filter down to your skin, then penetrate within, bringing the magick into you.

The chant can be the same, though depending on the situation you might want to replace "stroke" with another word. For example, if you are blending with a makeup sponge, you might want to use "pat." Also, if you are using foundation, instead of "and every color" say "of skin-toned color."

Conclusion

And there you have it! How to make magick with tattoos. This book has been the product of a hell of a lot of experimentation. I now pass the findings of my experiments off onto you all. I hope you take this system and add to it with your own experiments. And I sincerely hope when you find fun new things to do spiritually with tattoos that you tell others about it.

There are a couple things I would like you to remember as you take the information in this book and apply it to your life. First, have fun while you're getting your tattoo. Magick can be serious, and tattoos are permanent, yes, but life's too short not to have fun, and the positive energy you expend now will only bring more positivity to you down the road. There are more appropriate things to do if the situation is very serious. If you are faced with dire financial straits, find a cheaper spell. If you are very sick, don't give your body another thing to heal. If you are in active danger, spend all your time getting away from it.

Second, don't break the bank. Tattoos are "addicting." They also are expensive. If you are super excited about this system of magick but can only afford one or two, get one of those magickally versatile tattoos I talked about, and plan more specific tattoos for later. If you get something for just one intention, and you are prone to FOMO, you might come out saying you have to have four other tattoos for different things, and you want them now. Also, when you get your first magickal tattoo, experiment. Make sure this type of magick resonates with you—and that you've got the hang of it—before you move on to another tattoo.

The final thing I have to say is to be patient. This system is different from many other types of magick, and not just because it is expensive. I say this because the meaning behind the tattoo, and your connection to it, only becomes greater the more time you spend planning it and the more time and experiences you have with it. If you have twelve designs you want, you can space them out over five to six years to give each one time and attention. Also, spending as much time as you can or need with the design isn't just good for the magick. It's good to minimize regret, because you'll probably live with that tattoo for the rest of your life.

Outside of getting people to make magick with their tattoos, I came into this with two goals. One, to write the chapter on pain so at least one person would feel less squeamish. Two, to inspire more exploration on magick and body modification. There are so many kinds of body modification outside tattooing that I am not competent enough to teach. I hope to eventually learn from one of you, some day. If that happens, this book was a success.

May this book come into the hands of all who need it, all who want it, and all who may be inspired by it. Happy tattooing!

Acknowledgments

This book would never have seen the light of day if it weren't for my partner, Jay Dougherty. He listened to me complain while I was revising the first draft. He provided constructive feedback on who knows how many versions of this book with only moderately loud groaning. He has always inspired me.

Ash Yezuita, you have been one of my dearest friends and an unforgettable teacher. Thank you for sitting patiently through all the stressing out, providing encouragement, giving lots of feedback, and so many other things. I hope to one day see you on bookshelves, too.

Without Richard Webster's book *How to Write for the New Age Market,* I would never have had the nerve to write my first manuscript. None of this would have happened without him.

Elysia Gallo, I originally sent in a 90,000+ word manuscript on a completely unrelated topic that was quite niche. You could have stuck to a form rejection letter; instead you gave me a chance when I said I had other ideas. You were always completely responsive, kind, and patient with me as I navigated this (hopefully first) book. This book would not be half as good without you.

I wish to thank Andrea Neff and Marysa Storm for providing their feedback on the manuscript, Markus Ironwood for all the promotional opportunities he lined up, Shira Atakpu for her saintly patience going through all the photos I sent for the interior figures, Shannon McKuhen for designing the amazing cover, Toni Gallo for responding to all the questions I had about my contract, and all of the other amazing members of the Llewellyn support team whom I never had the distinct pleasure of meeting.

Marilyn Charles and Larry Davis allowed me to experiment on some of the contents of this book during my sessions with them, without hesitation. You both were instrumental to this work.

Tess Whitehurst, your support and advice are appreciated more than you know.

Chris Carter, you helped me make sure I didn't make a fool of myself with the photos of tattoo styles and gave some great advice. I hope to get a tattoo from you some day.

To Nathan, Holly, Sage, and arcanys_nyx: You were there for my social media journey from the very beginning, when I knew I had to commit to this to be a successful author. Your engagement carried me through even in the times I really just wanted to give up.

I'd like to thank all the other authors and content creators who have offered to help me promote the book, even in small ways. This will be submitted well before I see who follows through, so I can't name names. You know who you are, though.

I'd like to thank alcohol for softening the impact of my (first ever?) manuscript notes. Elysia, your debrief helped too!

Finally, I wanted to give a shout-out to my father for the book on the runes that was one of the first cobblestones down this path and to my mother for letting me put so many holes in the wall for the floating shelves for my childhood magickal book collection. I still maintain they were necessary.

Glossary

Altered state of consciousness: Any change in one's mental state from what is experienced as "normal" waking consciousness. Examples include daydreaming and trance.

Aphrodite: Greek goddess of love and beauty.

Apollo: Greek god of the sun, music, and prophecy.

Aspecting: The practice of bringing a deity or other spiritual being into one's body to take on the characteristics of that being and/or allow that being to speak through oneself.

Astral travel: The practice of separating one's consciousness from one's body to travel to other places or through other planes of existence.

Astrology: The practice of understanding human nature or predicting future events based on the position and movement of the planets and stars at a point in time.

Athame: A knife used as a magickal tool to direct energy.

Bindrune: A sigil made with runes.

Book of Shadows: A book or journal containing magickal notes and spells.

Brownie: A household spiritual being from Scottish folklore. It will come out at night and do chores for the house's family, as long as they leave an offering.

Carrier oil: The base oil in a blend into which the essential oils are diluted.

Cerberus: Three-headed dog who guards the entrance to the Greek Underworld.

Circle, the: A circular area made for magick with the purpose of containing the energy being raised and/or protecting from negative entities.

Cleanse and consecrate: The process of purifying a person, space, or object for magick by cleaning and then making sacred.

Correspondence: An association. In Witchcraft, frequently between an object and an intention.

Drawing down the moon: A magickal ritual in which a practitioner brings the power of the moon in themselves and aspects the goddess.

Elemental: A spirit associated with one of the four Persian elements: earth, air, fire, and water.

Fae, the: The race of fairies.

Flash: A pre-drawn tattoo design. You see them on the walls in tattoo studios frequently, often several together in a frame.

Flash sale: An event where a tattoo artist will offer discounted tattoos, almost always based on a select list of flash designs.

Freehand: A tattoo made without a stencil.

Glamour: A type of magick to change how people perceive oneself or make salient specific personality traits.

Gnome: Elemental of the element of earth.

Green Witch: A Witch whose practice prominently incorporates nature and things that come from nature.

Guardians of the Watchtowers: Spirits associated with the four directions, called upon to guard the circle or sacred space during rituals.

Hades: Greek god of the Underworld.

Hathor: Cow-headed Egyptian goddess of beauty, motherhood, and love.

Hecate: Greek goddess of magick.

Heka: Egyptian god of magick and medicine.

Hercules: Ancient Greek mythical hero.

Hugin and Munin: Two ravens belonging to Odin.

Intention: Desired outcome of a spell.

Isis: Egyptian goddess. Goddess of so many things modern practitioners frequently call upon her for any and all spells.

Linework: The outline of the tattoo; the lines that make up the design of the tattoo.

Mighty Dead, the: Spirits of Witches and Pagans who frequently are called upon to lend aid during a magickal working.

Morrigan, The: Celtic goddess of war, sovereignty, and prophecy.

Mortar and pestle: Device consisting of a bowl and a short, thick utensil used for grinding herbs.

Odin: Norse god of knowledge, poetry, magick, and wisdom. Hung from the World Tree for nine days and sacrificed an eye to receive the runes.

Oya: Yoruban goddess of winds and storms.

Pixie: A mischievous but usually good-natured spirit originating in the area of Devon and Cornwall, England.

Portfolio: A collection of the artist's work.

Reiki: A form of energy healing in which energy is channeled into the body through the hands.

Rune: Character from one of a few ancient Germanic alphabets. Each rune is believed to represent a concept that is usable in magick and divination.

Sachet: A small, sealed bag filled with spell ingredients.

Selene: Greek goddess of the moon.

Skyclad: Nude.

Sleeve: A tattoo or set of tattoos that covers a large part of the body, typically a limb.

Sleipnir: Eight-legged horse of Odin.

Stencil: An outline of the design either marked on the skin with a marker or printed out and transferred onto the skin.

Summoning Triangle: Part of the ritual setup for certain branches of ceremonial magick. Any spirits, angels, or demons summoned would appear in the triangle.

Sympathetic Magick: Magick that operates under the philosophy of "like attracts like," mimicking the result you want or using objects that symbolize the result you want to effect change.

Taglock: An item belonging to the recipient of a spell that binds the spell's effects to them.

Talisman: An object enchanted with magickal powers.

Theban: An alternative alphabetical system that is one of the most frequently utilized in magick.

Thor: Germanic god associated with lightning, protection, and the common people.

Trance: A half-conscious or deeply relaxed state of focus.

Visualization: The mental depiction of a spell's intention.

Wyrd: Norse concept of fate.

Yemaya: Yoruban goddess of the ocean, rivers, and motherhood.

Bibliography

Abbacan-Tuguic, Lalin, and Lunes Marnag. "Whatok (Tattooe): The Aesthetic Expression of Traditional Kalinga Beauty." *International Journal of Advanced Research in Management and Social Sciences* 5, no. 6 (2016): 725–39. https://www.garph.co.uk/IJARMSS/June2016/48.pdf.

Ankirskiy, Alexander. "Perception of Tattoos: Now and Then. Japan vs. the Western World." Bachelor's thesis, Iceland University, 2014. https://skemman.is/handle/1946/17199.

Antony, Mary Grace. "That's a Stretch: Reconstructing, Rearticulating, and Commodifying Yoga." *Frontiers in Communication* 3, no. 47 (2018). https://doi.org/10.3389/fcomm.2018.00047.

Atatsi, Eli Ayawo, Edem M. Azila-Gbettor, and Christopher Mensah. "Predicting Task Performance from Psychological Ownership and Innovative Work Behaviour: A Cross Sectional Study." *Cogent Business & Management* 8, no. 1 (2021): 1–15. https://doi.org/10.1080/23311975.2021.1917483.

Auryn, Mat. *Psychic Witch: A Metaphysical Guide to Meditation, Magick & Manifestation*. Llewellyn Publications, 2020.

Bertram, James Glass. *Flagellation & the Flagellants: A History of the Rod in All Countries, from the Earliest Period to the Present Time.* W. Reeves, 1904.

Bevilacqua, Daniela. "Embodying Sacred Pain: Practice of Austerities Among Hindu Ascetics." *South Asia: Journal of South Asian Studies* 48, no. 4 (2025): 804–23. https://doi.org/10.1080/00856401.2025.2524248.

Blackthorn, Amy. *Blackthorn's Botanical Magic: The Green Witch's Guide to Essential Oils for Spellcraft, Ritual, and Healing.* Weiser Books, 2018.

Bovin, Mette. *Nomads Who Cultivate Beauty: Wodaabe Dances and Visual Arts in Niger*. Nordic Africa Institute, 2001.

Bunn-Marcuse, Kathryn. "Wearing Identity: The Strength of Expression Through Personal Adornment." In *In the Spirit of the Ancestors: Contemporary Northwest Coast Art at the Burke Museum*, edited by Robin Kathleen Wright and Kathryn Bunn-Marcuse. University of Washington Press, 2013.

Caplan, Jane, ed. *Written on the Body: The Tattoo in European and American History*. Princeton University Press, 2000.

Cirillo, Andrew Nicholas. "Self-Flagellation as Sanctification in the Roman Catholic Church's Prelature of the Holy Cross and Opus Dei." *The Journal of Undergraduate Research* 10, no. 1 (2011): 8–12. https://www.rochester.edu/college/ugresearch/jur/wp-content/uploads/2024/05/2011-Fall.pdf.

Cook, Joanna. "Tattoos, Corporeality and the Self: Dissolving Borders in a Thai Monastery." *The Cambridge Journal of Anthropology* 27, no. 2 (2007): 20–35. https://www.jstor.org/stable/23820812.

Crow, Cairelle. *The Magic in Your Genes: Your Personal Path to Ancestor Work*. Weiser Books, 2023.

Cunningham, Sheila J., David J. Turk, Lynda M. Macdonald, and C. Neil Macrae. "Yours or Mine? Ownership and Memory." *Consciousness and Cognition* 17, no. 1 (2008): 312–8. https://doi.org/10.1016/j.concog.2007.04.003.

Deter-Wolf, Aaron, Tanya M. Peres, and Steven Karacic. "Ancient Native American Bone Tattooing Tools and Pigments: Evidence from Central Tennessee." *Journal of Archaeological Science: Reports* 37 (2021). https://doi.org/10.1016/j.jasrep.2021.103002.

Deter-Wolf, Aaron, Benoît Robitaille, Lars Krutak, and Sébastien Galliot. "The World's Oldest Tattoos." *Journal of Archaeological Science: Reports* 5 (2016): 19–24. https://doi.org/10.1016/j.jasrep.2015.11.007.

Dutta, Subhankar. "'Becoming Someone Else': Formation of Identities and Representations in the Folk Rituals of Hook Swinging (*Gajan*) Festival." In *The Dynamics of Folklore and Orature in Culture*, edited by Pallavi Mishra. Vishvanatha Kaviraja Institute, 2021. https://www.scribd.com/document/521267646/The-Dynamics-of-Folklore-and-Orature-in-Culture-Pallavi-Mishra-Ed-Copy.

Easton, Dossie, and Janet W. Hardy. *Radical Ecstasy*. Greenery Press, 2015.

Echols, Damien, and Lorri Davis. *Ritual: An Essential Grimoire*. Sounds True, 2022.

Egan, Keith. "Being with Others: Croagh Patrick in July 2008." *Irish Journal of Anthropology* 14 (2011): 14–18. https://www.academia.edu/29804715/Special_Issue_The_Value_of_Ethnographic_Writing_IJA.

Englert, Julia Valerie. "What Is 'Mere' About the Mere Ownership Effect? The Role of Semantic Processes for the Self's Impact on Memory." PhD diss., University of Saarland, 2018.

Furey, Louise. "Archaeological Evidence for Tattooing in Polynesia and Micronesia." In *Ancient Ink: The Archaeology of Tattooing*, edited by Lars Krutak and Aaron Deter-Wolf. University of Washington Press, 2017.

Gatrad, Abdul Rashid, and Aziz Sheikh. "Hajj: Journey of a Lifetime." *BMJ* 330 (2005): 133. https://doi.org/10.1136/bmj.330.7483.133.

Glucklich, Ariel. *Sacred Pain: Hurting the Body for the Sake of the Soul.* Oxford University Press, 2003.

Griswold, Eliza. *I Am the Beggar of the World: Landays from Contemporary Afghanistan*. Macmillan, 2014.

Hambly, Wilfrid Dyson. *The History of Tattooing.* Dover Publications, 2009.

Handy, Willowdean Chatterson. *Tattooing in the Marquesas.* Vol. 1. The Bernice P. Bishop Museum, 1922. https://hbs.bishopmuseum.org/pubs-online/pdf/bull1.pdf.

Herkes, Michael. *Glamstrology: Discover Your Signature Style with Astrology*. Llewellyn Publications, 2024.

Islam, Thowhidul. "Fasting in Hinduism, Buddhism and Islam: A Comparative Study." *Journal of Islamic Studies* 2, no. 3 (2024): 156–68. https://maqolat.com/index.php/i/article/view/74/35.

Jang, Thomas. "Would Cultures: Ainu Tattoos." Ubique: American Geographical Society. Accessed August 2025. https://ubiqueags.org/world-cultures-ainu-tattoos/.

Jennings, Ken. *100 Places to See After You Die: A Travel Guide to the Afterlife*. Simon and Schuster, 2023.

Jerrentrup, Maja Tabea. "The Body, the Spirit, and the Other: Yantras as Embodied Cultural Integration." *Social Sciences* 13, no. 1 (2024): 34. https://doi.org/10.3390/socsci13010034.

Kaeppler, Adrienne L. "Tattooed Beauty: A Pacific Case Study." *AnthroNotes* 22, no. 2 (2001): 9–13.

Krutak, Lars. "Embodied Symbols of the South Seas: Tattoo in Polynesia." Lars Krutak. June 3, 2013. https://larskrutak.com/embodied-symbols-of-the-south-seas-tattoo-in-polynesia/.

Krutak, Lars. *Indigenous Tattoo Traditions: A History of Humanity Through Skin and Ink*. Princeton University Press, 2025.

Krutak, Lars. "In the Realm of Spirits: Traditional Dayak Tattoo in Borneo." Lars Krutak. November 23, 2012. https://larskrutak.com/in-the-realm-of-spirits-traditional-dayak-tattoo-in-borneo/.

Krutak, Lars. "Losing Your Head Among the Tattooed Headhunters of Taiwan." Lars Krutak. November 23, 2012. https://larskrutak.com/loosing-your-head-among-the-tattooed-headhunters-of-taiwan/.

Krutak, Lars. "Naga Tattoos of Myanmar." Lars Krutak. August 16, 2019. https://larskrutak.com/naga-tattoos-of-myanmar/.

Krutak, Lars. *Spiritual Skin: Magical Tattoos and Scarification: Wisdom, Healing, Shamanic Power, Protection*. Editions Reuss, 2013.

Krutak, Lars. *Tattoo Traditions of Asia: Ancient and Contemporary Expressions of Identity*. University of Hawaii Press, 2024.

Krutak, Lars. "Therapeutic Tattooing in the Arctic: Ethnographic, Archaeological, and Ontological Frameworks of Analysis." *International Journal of Paleopathology* 25 (2019): 99–109. https://doi.org/10.1016/j.ijpp.2018.05.003.

Kynes, Sandra. *Llewellyn's Complete Book of Correspondences: A Comprehensive & Cross-Referenced Resource for Pagans & Wiccans.* Llewellyn Publications, 2013.

Lipp, Deborah. *Magical Power for Beginners: How to Raise & Send Energy for Spells that Work.* Llewellyn Publications, 2017.

Lippert, Paul. "Tattooing: The Image Becomes the Self." *ETC: A Review of General Semantics* 37, no. 2 (1980): 158–71.

Longchar, Resenmenla. "Rites of Passage: Special Reference to Ao-Naga Puberty Rites as Markers of Identity." *Litinfinite Journal* 2, no. 2 (2020): 36–49. https://doi.org/10.47365/litinfinite.2.2.2020.36-49.

Mankey, Jason, Matt Cavalli, Amanda Lynn, and Ari Mankey. *The Witch's Book of Spellcraft: A Practical Guide to Connecting with the Magick of Candles, Crystals, Plants & Herbs.* Llewellyn Publications, 2022.

Nolan, Barbara. *A Year of Pagan Prayer: A Sourcebook of Poems, Hymns, and Invocations from Four Thousand Years of Pagan History.* Llewellyn Publications, 2021.

Perkins, Andrew, and Mark R. Forehand. "Implicit Self-Referencing: The Effect of Nonvolitional Self-Association on Brand and Product Attitude." *Journal of Consumer Research* 39, no. 1 (2012): 142–56.

Pike, Dree Amandi. *The Art of Aromatherapy in Magick: A Guide for the Modern Witch.* Llewellyn Publications, 2024.

Poznik, G. David, Brenna M. Henn, Muh-Ching Yee, Elizbieta Sliwerska, Ghia M. Euskirchen, Alice A. Lin, Michael Snyder, Lluis Quintana-Murci, Jeffrey M. Kidd, Peter A. Underhill, and Carlos D. Bustamante. "Sequencing Y Chromosomes Resolves Discrepancy in Time to Common Ancestor of Males Versus Females."

Science 341, no. 6145 (2013): 562–65. https://doi.org/10.1126/science.1237619.

Rada, Julie. "Extremely Up-in-the-Air: Flesh Hook Suspension and Performance." In *Pain Without Boundaries: Inquiries Across Cultures*, edited by Roy F. Fox and Nicole Monteiro. Brill, 2014.

RavenWolf, Silver. *Solitary Witch: The Ultimate Book of Shadows for the New Generation*. Llewellyn Publications, 2003.

RavenWolf, Silver. *To Ride a Silver Broomstick: New Generation Witchcraft*. Llewellyn Publications, 1993.

Rosecrans, Jennipher A. "Wearing the Universe: Symbolic Markings in Early Modern England." In *Written on the Body: The Tattoo in European and American History*, edited by Jane Caplan. Princeton University Press, 2000.

Rubel, Nora L. "The Feast at the End of the Fast: The Evolution of an American Jewish Ritual." In *Tastes of Faith: Jewish Eating in the United States*, edited by Steven J. Ross, Leah Hochman, and Lisa Ansell. Purdue University Press, 2017. https://docs.lib.purdue.edu/cgi/viewcontent.cgi?article=1008&context=casden.

Rush, John A. *Spiritual Tattoo: A Cultural History of Tattooing, Piercing, Scarification, Branding, and Implants*. Frog Books, 2005.

"Sak Yant Information." Thai Tattoo Café. Accessed October 12, 2025. https://thaitattoocafe.com/sak-yant-information.

Sanders, Clinton, and D. Angus Vail. *Customizing the Body: The Art and Culture of Tattooing*. Temple University Press, 2008.

Schaeffer, Katherine, and Shradha Dinesh. "32% of Americans Have a Tattoo, Including 22% Who Have More Than One." Pew Research Center. August 15, 2023. https://www.pewresearch.org/short-reads/2023/08/15/32-of-americans-have-a-tattoo-including-22-who-have-more-than-one/.

Scharbrodt, Oliver. "Contesting Ritual Practices in Twelver Shiism: Modernism, Sectarianism and the Politics of Self-Flagellation (*Taṭbīr*)." *British Journal of Middle Eastern Studies* 50, no. 5 (2023): 1067–90. https://doi.org/10.1080/13530194.2022.2057279.

Shishlina, Natalia I., E. V. Belkevich, and A. N. Usachuk. "Bronze Age Tattoos: Sympathetic Magic or Decoration?" In *Tattoos and Body Modifications in Antiquity: Proceedings of the Sessions at the Annual Meetings of the European Association of Archaeologist in the Hague and Oslo* vol. 9 (2013): 67–74. https://www.researchgate.net/publication/271587804_Bronze_Age_Tattoos_Sympathetic_Magic_or_Decoration.

Siegel, Laure. "India on the Road: Part 4." *Inkers Magazine*. Accessed October 15, 2025. https://inkers.app/en-US/mag/category/tattoopedia/content/152.

Siloam Hospitals Medical Team. "Causes and Treatments of Abdominal Pain During Fasting." Siloam. August 21, 2024. https://www.siloamhospitals.com/en/informasi-siloam/artikel/causes-and-treatments-of-abdominal-pain-during-fasting-.

Spier, Leslie. *The Sun Dance of the Plains Indians: Its Development and Diffusion*. Vol. 16, part 7 of *Anthropological Papers of the American Museum of Natural History*. The Trustees, 1921.

"Tattoo Tourism: Why Nepal Is the Next Big Spot for Ink Lovers?" Amazing Nepal Trek & Expedition. May 14, 2025. https://www.amazingnepaltrek.com/blog/tattoo-tourism-why-nepal-is-the-next-big-spot-for-ink-lovers.

Vandermeersch, Patrick. "Self-Flagellation in the Early Modern Era." In *The Sense of Suffering: Constructions of Physical Pain in Early Modern Culture*, edited by Jan Frans van Dijkhuizen and

Karl A. E. Enenkel. Brill, 2009. https://doi.org/10.1163/ej.9789004172470.i-520.50.

Ward, Colleen. "Thaipusam in Malaysia: A Psycho-Anthropological Analysis of Ritual Trance, Ceremonial Possession and Self-Mortification Practices." *Ethos* 12, no. 4 (1984): 307–34. https://www.jstor.org/stable/639977.

Wiley, Kristi L. "Supernatural Powers and Their Attainment in Jainism." In *Yoga Powers: Extraordinary Capacities Attained Through Meditation and Concentration*, edited by Knut A. Jacobsen. Brill, 2012.

Zakroff, Laura Tempest. *Sigil Witchery: A Witch's Guide to Crafting Magick Symbols*. Llewellyn Publications, 2018.

Index

G

I

M

O

P

R

V

W

To Write to the Author

If you wish to contact the author or would like more information about this book, please write to the author in care of Llewellyn Worldwide Ltd. and we will forward your request. Both the author and the publisher appreciate hearing from you and learning of your enjoyment of this book and how it has helped you. Llewellyn Worldwide Ltd. cannot guarantee that every letter written to the author can be answered, but all will be forwarded. Please write to:

Jake Morningstar
℅ Llewellyn Worldwide
2143 Wooddale Drive
Woodbury, MN 55125-2989

Please enclose a self-addressed stamped envelope for reply, or $1.00 to cover costs. If outside the U.S.A., enclose an international postal reply coupon.

Many of Llewellyn's authors have websites with additional information and resources. For more information, please visit our website at https://www.llewellyn.com.